❧[A Bead in Time]❧

D1533402

A Bead in time

35 jewelry projects inspired by slices of life

Lisa Crone

Northern Plains Public Library
Ault Colorado

NORTH LIGHT BOOKS
Cincinnati, Ohio
www.mycraftivity.com

A Bead in Time. Copyright © 2010 by Lisa Crone. Manufactured in China. All rights reserved. The patterns and drawings in the book are for personal use of reader. By permission of the author and publisher, they may be either hand-traced or photocopied to make single copies, but under no circumstances may they be resold or republished. It is permissible for the purchaser to make the projects contained herein and sell them at fairs, bazaars and craft shows. No other part of this book may be reproduced in any form or by any electronic or mechanical means including information storage and retrieval systems without permission in writing from the publisher, except by a reviewer, who may quote a brief passage in review. Published by North Light Books, an imprint of F+W Media, Inc., 4700 East Galbraith Road, Cincinnati, Ohio 45236. (800) 289-0963. First edition.

14 13 12 11 10   5 4 3 2 1

Distributed in Canada by Fraser Direct
100 Armstrong Avenue
Georgetown, ON, Canada L7G 5S4
Tel: (905) 877-4411

Distributed in the U.K. and Europe by David & Charles
Brunel House, Newton Abbot, Devon, TQ12 4PU, England
Tel: (+44) 1626 323200, Fax: (+44) 1626 323319
E-mail: postmaster@davidandcharles.co.uk

Distributed in Australia by Capricorn Link
P.O. Box 704, S. Windsor, NSW 2756 Australia
Tel: (02) 4577-3555

Library of Congress
Cataloging-in-Publication Data
Crone, Lisa
  A bead in time / Lisa Crone.
    p. cm.
  Includes index.
  ISBN-13: 978-1-60061-310-4 (pbk. : alk. paper)
  ISBN-10: 1-60061-310-1 (pbk. : alk. paper)
  1. Jewelry making. 2. Beadwork. I. Title.
  TT212.C785 2009
  739.27--dc22
                        2009026854

Editors: Julie Hollyday and Rachel Scheller
Designer: Corrie Schaffeld
Production Coordinator: Greg Nock
Photographer: Christine Polomsky, David Peterson
Photo Stylist: Nora Martini

METRIC CONVERSION CHART

to convert	to	multiply by
Inches	Centimeters	2.54
Centimeters	Inches	0.4
Feet	Centimeters	30.5
Centimeters	Feet	0.03
Yards	Meters	0.9
Meters	Yards	1.1
Sq. Inches	Sq. Centimeters	6.45
Sq. Centimeters	Sq. Inches	0.16
Sq. Feet	Sq. Meters	0.09
Sq. Meters	Sq. Feet	10.8
Sq. Yards	Sq. Meters	0.8
Sq. Meters	Sq. Yards	1.2
Pounds	Kilograms	0.45
Kilograms	Pounds	2.2
Ounces	Grams	28.3
Grams	Ounces	0.035

Dedication

My sincere thanks to the universe for providing the inspiration for this book.

Acknowledgments

I would like to thank my husband for his kind and continual support throughout this process and always! Thanks to my friends and family, whose encouragement means more to me than they probably realize. I'm also thankful to have worked with such a wonderful publishing company. The ever-supportive and kind mentoring from acquisitions editor Tonia Davenport, and the sweet, "easy-peasy" attitude of editor Julie Hollyday; both have been such a pleasure to work with. Thanks to Christine Polomsky, who, in addition to a being a world-renowned photographer, also has a natural talent for putting people at ease and creating a relaxed work atmosphere.

About the Author

Lisa Crone has been designing beaded jewelry for more than eighteen years. She is a self-professed bead fanatic and enjoys learning new techniques from other bead enthusiasts through books, magazines and classes. Lisa currently maintains a daily beading blog at www.abeadaday.blogspot.com where the tagline reads, "Appreciating the individual beauty of beads and the unique works of art they are used to create!"

Table *of* Contents

Introduction

I have found that regardless of a beader's experience or expertise level, we all have moments of "beader's block" when it comes to design. I can't tell you how many times I have pulled out beads feeling excited about what I was going to create, only to become discouraged hours later when my projects didn't turn out. My vision of something unique or unusual somehow found its way back to the traditional or typical.

During one of these frustrating periods, I happened to be looking through old vacation photos. I found a picture of Niagara Falls and wondered if I could make a bracelet that resembled the falls. It had been a great trip, and I wanted a piece of jewelry to remind me of it. I had fun treasure hunting for just the right beads, and I successfully interpreted the beauty of the falls into a sparkly piece of jewelry. It was then that I realized I had an untapped source of inspiration in my vacation photos. That was the beginning of this process, and I wanted to share these ideas with my fellow beaders. Throughout this book, you can follow my journey as I challenged myself to see the world in a different way and find inspiration around every corner.

The fun begins when you select a subject to work with and decide how you would like to interpret it. The subject you select will often dictate the direction to take. Create your subject literally, by making an obvious replication of it, or in the abstract, by using colors, fibers or other materials that remind you of the item.

Treasure hunting for beads is the next step. Take time to search through your own bead collection, or head to your favorite bead and craft stores. Depending on your subject, you might find what you need in other places, such as the grocery or hardware stores. Be on the lookout for items that can be interpreted into your designs and will help you achieve the look you desire.

It is helpful to find your beads first and then determine the technique you will use to pull the design together. Use your imagination and sketch out how you would like the beads to be arranged. You might even invent a new technique, depending on what you are trying to bring to life. There is no right or wrong in this process—just have fun!

If you can't wrap your mind around this concept right away, but still feel the need to break out of a beading rut, take a look at chapter four for some alternate methods of finding inspiration. Using other craft materials in your jewelry projects, such as appliqués, buttons or ribbon, is a great way to get started. Sometimes you just need to take that first step from the ordinary to let your creativity take over.

Since it worked for me, I am hoping this simple concept will inspire and challenge you to consider a new method for creating jewelry. By taking inspiration from the things around you and interpreting them into a piece of jewelry, you are capturing those thoughts, occasions or sights into wearable keepsakes. Start by thinking of the things you love, the vacations you have taken, the food you eat, the sun in the sky, the flowers in your garden or your favorite work of art—the possibilities are endless, so make a challenging game out of it.

Materials and Tools

There are an amazing array of materials and tools for jewelry making, and new products arrive on the scene daily! Most of what you choose to use is a matter of personal preference and taste. However, the basic materials and tools are listed below.

MATERIALS

BEADS are anything you can string or wire onto a piece of jewelry. No rules apply!

CRIMP BEADS AND TUBES are used to connect a clasp to beading wire.

BEADING WIRE comes in many forms, the most common being nylon-coated steel, which comes in a variety of weights and colors.

 The size or weight of the beads you use dictates the type of wire needed. Most pieces work well with .012" (.3mm) diameter–.015" (.4mm).

CRAFT WIRE comes in many colors and gauges. Most common are 20-gauge to 26-gauge. The larger the number, the thinner the wire.

JUMP RINGS are metal loops made in a variety of sizes. They are used as connectors by opening and closing the loops.

SPLIT RINGS are metal loops in a variety of sizes that are used as connectors, similar to key rings. They feature two continuous loops that secure beads or other findings with no chance of opening.

CLASPS are made in many styles and designs. Most common are the lobster clasp and toggle clasp. Each jewelry design will usually dictate the type of clasp that seems appropriate for the piece. If not, I usually use a lobster clasp due to its simple styling and secure connection. The toggle clasp is a loop with a bar that slides through it and catches to secure the piece.

FIRELINE is a very fine, but strong beading thread that is also manufactured as fishing line. This product comes in sizes .06mm to .15mm or 1lb test to 6lb test in both crystal and smoke colors.

MONOFILAMENT OR CLEAR LINE comes in a variety of sizes based on the strength or diameter needed. Clear line is used in pieces where it is important to the design that the thread be invisible.

HEADPINS have either a flat or decorative end on them to stop beads and are used for making dangles or earrings.

EYEPINS are similar to a headpin, but have a loop at one end for making easy connections.

TOOLS

BEADING NEEDLES come in a variety of lengths and diameters. I like to use the smallest diameter and longest length. These needles typically bend easily for maneuvering in and out of small beads.

MEMORY WIRE CUTTERS are specifically for memory wire because of its heavy gauge. Other cutting tools can be used, but will often damage the cutting surface.

WIRE CUTTERS come in a variety of sizes and strengths, but for most jobs, a standard 4½" wire cutter or nipper will do.

FLUSH CUTTERS allow you to cut down to the point of the cutter so you can get into small spaces. They are great for cutting the beading wire tail after the final crimp has been made.

ROUND-NOSE PLIERS are used for making rounded loops in wire.

NEEDLE-NOSE PLIERS are great for flattening crimps in tight spaces.

CRIMPING PLIERS have two grooves for making the two-step round or folded crimp.

Basic Techniques

The following techniques are used to create a wide variety of jewelry pieces. If you are new to jewelry making, you might be surprised to find that each one can be mastered easily with a little practice. The simplest of these techniques, making a loop, is all you need to know to make a memory wire bracelet or a simple pair of earrings.

Using Crimp Beads or Tubes

Crimp beads or tubes are used to connect a clasp to beading wire. Crimps can also be used on decorative beading wire above and below beads to hold them in place.

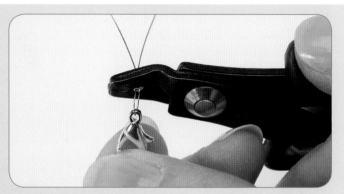

1. Crimp tube

Thread the wires through the crimp bead or tube. Make sure the wires aren't crossed. Using the crimping pliers, place the bead or tube in the groove closest to the handle and squeeze.

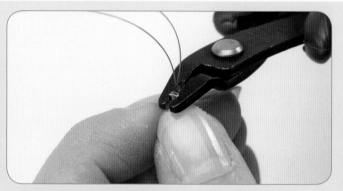

2. Flatten crimp

Move the crimp bead or tube into the other slot. Press down to round out the tube.

Flattening Crimp Beads or Tubes

Crimp beads or tubes can be flattened in any project, and it is often a personal decision whether to flatten or make a two-step crimp. However, at the end of some beading projects, there might not be enough space to use the crimping pliers. Using needle-nose pliers is the perfect solution for flattening a crimp in a tight space.

Tying an Overhand Knot

An overhand knot technique is used when stringing materials such as hemp cord, monofilament or Fireline to secure the beadwork.

1. Flatten tube

Thread the wire through the crimp tube. Make sure the wires are not crossed. Using the needle-nose pliers, flatten the tube.

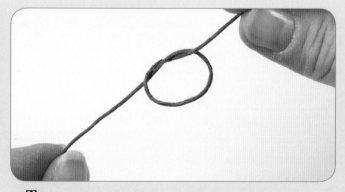

1. Tie knot

Form a loop in the cording, cross it over itself and bring one end over and through the loop. Pull the ends tight

MAKING A LOOP

This technique is used often in jewelry making, especially when making earrings or dangles.

1. BEND WIRE

Using your hands or a pair of needle-nose pliers, bend the wire to a 90° angle.

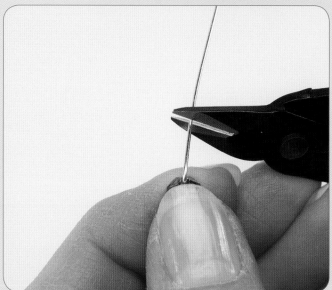

2. TRIM WIRE

Using your finger, measure approximately ⅜" (1cm) above the bead. Use the wire cutters to trim any excess wire.

3. FORM LOOP

Using the round-nose pliers, form the loop.

MAKING A WIRE-WRAPPED LOOP

Wire-wrapped loops are used for decorative purposes or in situations where the wire would come loose if a plain loop was used. The wrapped loop provides more security.

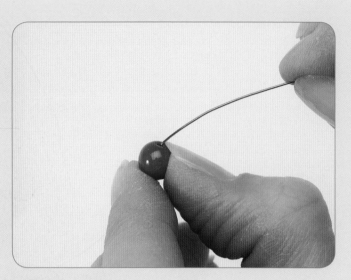

1. BEND WIRE
Using your fingers, bend the wire at a 90° angle.

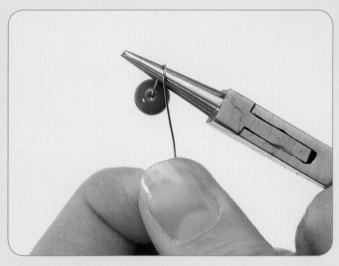

2. MAKE LOOP
Using the round-nose pliers, make a loop.

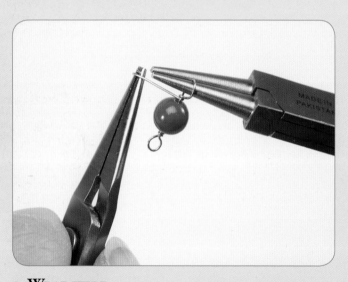

3. WRAP WIRE
Keep the round-nose pliers in the loop. Using the needle-nose pliers, grasp the wire tail and twist it around the base of the loop several times.

4. TRIM EXCESS WIRE
Using the wire cutters, trim the excess wire.

CONNECTING SPLIT RINGS

If a dangle is being placed on the finished piece, a split ring is connected to allow the dangle to hang properly. You can also use split rings as the connector piece with lobster claw clasps; the split ring won't pull apart like some jump rings.

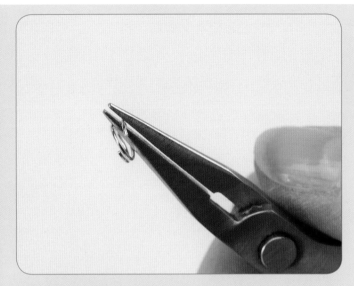

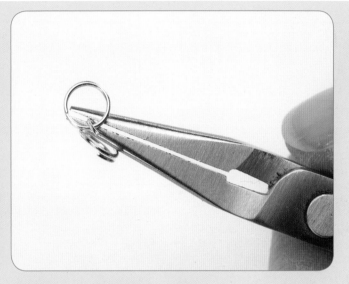

1. OPEN RING
Using the needle-nose pliers, open one end of the split ring.

2. THREAD ON SECOND RING
Thread on the other split ring. Work it through the first split ring as you would put a key on a key ring.

OPENING AND CLOSING JUMP RINGS

Jump rings are commonly used in jewelry making. It is important to open and close jump rings correctly to prevent breakage.

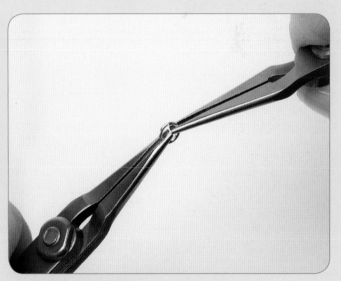

1. OPEN JUMP RING
Using two sets of needle-nose pliers, open the jump ring by bringing one set of pliers toward you.

2. CLOSE JUMP RING
Reverse the previous step to close the jump ring.

Chapter 1: Metro Mixes

Many of the projects in this chapter were inspired by architectural and geometric designs. You can learn a lot about yourself when you compile photos of objects that catch your eye. I find I am drawn to both circular and crisp, linear patterns. The more I look around my environment, I can see how I have surrounded myself with these patterns and believe they must be important to my well-being.

Each of these projects is unique in its construction because it is based on the object that inspired it. This chapter is filled with projects that were designed using methods I had never tried before. I drew on my existing skills and knowledge of materials. Memory wire, one of my favorite materials, is incorporated in different ways to create the *Golden Gate Bridge* (see page 24), *Chinatown* (see page 28) and *Wrought Iron Fence* (see page 32) bracelets. Basic stringing knowledge was the basis for *Frank Lloyd Wright* (see page 35). The square stitch was used to create *City Style* (see page 18). This project is great for those who enjoy working with a needle and thread.

Once you begin designing jewelry in this manner, you will quickly discover the architectural or artistic beauty in objects you come across every day. It's a great experiment in appreciation and gratitude, which always improves your out-look whether you need it or not.

City Style

I love old brick buildings and sleek, geometric buildings, too. This is my favorite of all the buildings I see during my downtown workday. I thought it would be fun and challenging to make it into a piece of jewelry. Working with these hematite cubes was a lot like building my own skyscraper.

MATERIALS

28 4mm × 4mm brushed pewter cubes

26 4mm × 4mm hematite cubes

43 twisted black bugle beads

86 pewter-lined seed beads

.012" (.3mm)–.015" (.4mm) beading wire

Fireline or beading thread

1 silver lobsterclaw clasp

2 split rings

2 crimp beads

TOOLS

wire cutters

beading needle

crimping tool

FINISHED LENGTH:
16½" (50cm)

GET INSPIRED!

Do you find yourself turning on autopilot occasionally? Passing by the same sites every day often turns on this mechanism. If you are willing to try this experiment, select a day and commit to really seeing the sites you come across on your way to work, school or the shopping center. It helps to have your camera or cell phone handy just in case you find yourself inspired!

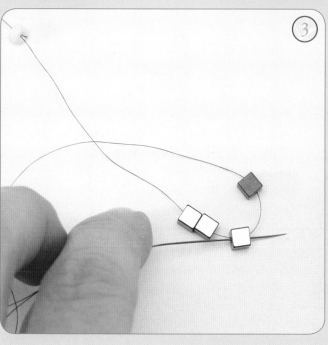

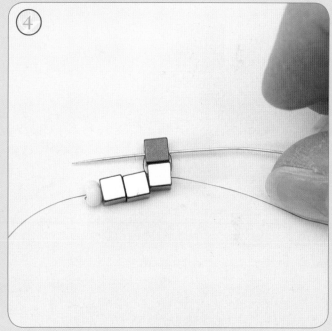

1. Add stop bead

Cut a 2½' (1m) piece of Fireline. Add a stop bead to one end, leaving a 6" (15cm) tail for knotting and finishing.

2. String on hematite cubes

Add three hematite cubes. These form the first row of one side of the building.

3. Add cube

Add one brushed pewter cube. Hold the brushed pewter cube on top of the end bead of the first row. Take the needle through the bead below it.

4. Secure cube

The thread should be coming out to the right of the first row. Now, take the needle up and back through the pewter bead, from right to left.

5. BEGIN PATTERN

Following Steps 1 and 2, complete the following pattern:

    Row 1: three hematite cubes

    Row 2: two hematite cubes, one pewter cube

    Row 3: two hematite cubes, one pewter cube

    Row 4: three hematite cubes

    Row 5: three pewter cubes

    Row 6: three hematite cubes

    Row 7: three pewter cubes

    Row 8: three pewter cubes

    Row 9: two pewter cubes

    Row 10: one pewter cube

There are two beads in the ninth row and one bead in the tenth row. To manage the decrease, instead of taking the needle up to the ninth row, move it down to the seventh row, through the bead below the last bead on the seventh row. Then bring it out between the first and second bead on the seventh row.

TIP

As beads are added, pull on the Fireline gently to secure them in place.

6. FINISH ROW 8

Take the needle up through the middle bead in the eighth row continuing through the third bead in the eighth row (from right to left).

7. BEGIN ROW 9

Thread should be coming out the right side of the eighth row. Add a pewter cube to the ninth row, sewing it to the cube below it in the eighth row as usual. Add the second bead in the ninth row, sewing it to the cube below it in the eighth row as usual.

    Make one extra half stitch by going back through the cube below the center bead in the eighth row and bring the needle out between the second and third bead in the eighth row.

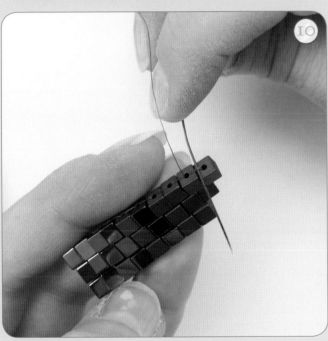

8. FINISH ROW 9
Take the needle up through the end bead on the ninth row (from left to right). Thread should be coming out the left side of the cube.

9. ADD ROW 10
Add the final bead in the tenth row by sewing it to the cube below it in the ninth row.

10. SECURE BEADS
Secure wobbly areas by adding stitches as needed and bring the needle out one of the end beads. Then put the needle under the thread that is securing two rows. Make an overhand knot (see Tying an Overhand Knot on page 12). Give one last tug (which, in some cases, can help the knot to disappear into the beads) and weave the tail back through the beads. Trim any excess.

11. BEGIN JOINING THE TWO SIDES
Repeat Steps 1–10 to create the other half of the building. Add Fireline to the needle if necessary, and tie it onto the thread outside row 1 on one side of the building. Run the needle through all the beads on the bottom row. Add a seed bead, and run the needle through the bottom row of the other side of the building. Pull the line tight and knot the thread to the side as if tying off. Take the needle back through the bottom row, seed bead and bottom row of the other side. Knot on the outside of the row.

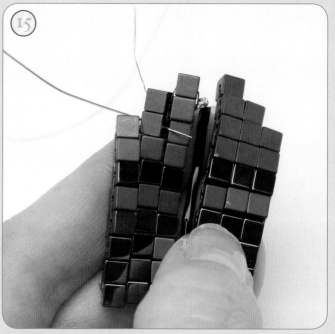

12. PREPARE TO ADD BUGLE BEADS
Bring the needle back through half of the bottom row and the seed bead.

13. THREAD ON BUGLE BEADS
Thread on the three bugle beads and a seed bead.

14. TAKE THREAD THROUGH ROW 9
Insert the needle through both beads in row 9 on one side.

15. SECURE BEADS
Tie an overhand knot to secure the beads. Bring the needle down through the second bead on row 8.

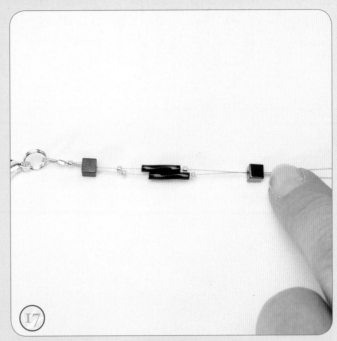

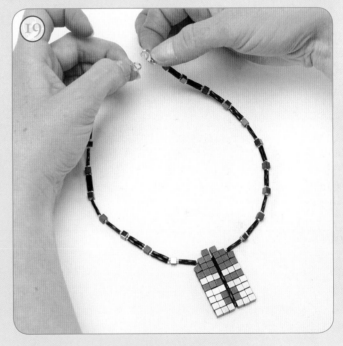

16. JOIN BUILDING SIDES

Bring the needle up through the center bead on row 9. Go through the seed bead and through row 9 on the other half of the building. Secure the building by tying an overhand knot. Trim any excess wire using sharp scissors or a cutting tool.

17. BEGIN NECKLACE

Cut two 19" (48cm) pieces of beading wire. Secure the wire using a crimp tube and lobsterclaw clasp over both strands (see Using Crimp Beads or Tubes on page 12).

Add a seed bead over both wires. Begin the following pattern:

  Pewter cube over both wires

  Seed bead, bugle bead and seed bead, on each strand

  Hematite cube over both wires

18. CONNECT PENDANT TO NECKLACE

Continue the pattern in Step 17 until you have used ten cubes. After the last combination of beads, run both wires through row 9 of the building including going through the seed bead. (This might take some work.)

19. COMPLETE NECKLACE

On the other side of the building, repeat the pattern in Step 17 until you have used ten cubes. Add a seed bead over both wires. Add a seed bead, crimp and split ring over both wires and crimp into place (see Connecting Split Rings on page 15).

Golden Gate Bridge

The first "real" vacation my husband and I took was to San Francisco. The Golden Gate Bridge is an awesome sight—the color is so bold! After looking through these vacation photos, I knew I wanted to re-create this structure as a reminder of the trip. When I found these brightly colored beads, I started thinking about using memory wire and wrapping "poles" of beaded wires between two memory-wire supports to replicate the look of the bridge.

MATERIALS
112 Toho copper triangle seed beads

8–10g Toho copper 11/0 round seed beads

16" (41cm) memory wire

5' (2m) 24-gauge copper wire

TOOLS
memory wire cutters

standard wire cutters

needle-nose pliers

round-nose pliers

FINISHED LENGTH:
7½" (19cm)

GET INSPIRED!

Have you ever found yourself in awe of architectural structures that seem to be a feat of physics? You may have encountered sights like this in your travels or even your own backyard. Imagine integrating the look of one of these structures into a wearable object. It would certainly make a great conversation piece!

1. Prepare memory wire

Cut two 8" (20cm) pieces of memory wire. Use round-nose pliers to turn one end of each piece of wire into a loop. Cut an 18" (46cm) piece of 24-gauge wire. Hold the two pieces of memory wire together at the loops and run the copper wire through both loops. Wrap them together tightly.

2. Add beads

Using wire cutters, trim any excess wire. On each strand of memory wire, add two round seed beads and five triangle seed beads.

3. Begin coil

Using wire cutters, cut a 2' (1m) piece of 24-gauge wire. Hold the memory wire strands approximately ¾" (2cm) apart. Center the 24-gauge wire to the memory wire. Wrap one side of the wire around the memory wire to secure it. Repeat for the other side.

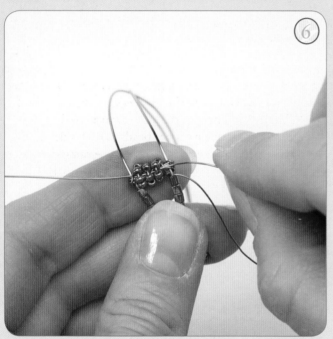

4. WRAP COLUMN

Holding the two pieces of memory wire approximately ¾" (2cm) apart, wrap the 24-gauge wire around the two pieces five times to form a column.

5. MAKE COIL

Add ten round seed beads to the same piece of 24-gauge wire and wrap the beaded strand around the column.

6. COMPLETE COIL

Feed the wire ends through the beaded coil. Twist the excess wire between the coils if necessary. Using the wire cutters, trim the excess wire.

7. FINISH BRACELET

Add five triangle seed beads to each strand of memory wire, holding the two wires in one hand at the desired height (approximately ½" [1cm] apart for column 2).

For each successive wrap, the column height will increase slightly, requiring more round beads for wrapping. Columns 7 through 11 will decrease in height to mirror the beginning columns.

After wrapping the final column, add five triangle seed beads and two round seed beads to each memory wire and turn the ends into loops

Cut a piece of 24-gauge wire 18" (46cm) long and run it through both loops. Wrap the loops together tightly as you did in Step 1. Using the wire cutters, trim any excess wire.

Variation: Golden Gate Bridge Earrings

I wanted to make a pair of earrings to go with this bracelet, continuing the coil wrapping for consistency in the design. I love how the bead color is true to the color in the vacation photo. It really takes me back there.

MATERIALS

16" (41cm) 20-gauge copper wire

2' (61cm) 24-gauge copper wire

4' (122cm) 26-gauge copper wire

34 Toho copper triangle seed beads

50 Toho copper 11/0 round seed beads

1. CREATE BEADED COIL DANGLE

Cut approximately 2' (61cm) of 26-gauge copper wire. Bring the ends together and form an oval shape using one point of the needle-nose pliers. Use one end of the wire to wrap around the neck of the loop and then begin "sewing" the wire around the oval. When the loop is covered, wrap once around the neck of the loop. Add approximately 20 round copper beads to the longest remaining strand of wire. Using shorter remaining wire as the "column," wrap the beaded wire around the strand four times. When completely wrapped and pulled tight, gently twist the two raw ends of wire together once or twice and feed one length of wire up through the earring. Trim any excess wire.

2. CREATE OVAL RING FOR DANGLE

Cut a 1' (30cm) piece of 24-gauge wire. Put the ends together and add the beaded coil dangle to the center. Using your finger in the loop, form an oval shape. Add eight triangle copper beads to each side of the wire and twist the ends together. Use round-nose pliers to make a loop with remaining wire that will be used to connect an ear wire. Wrap wire ends around neck of the loop and trim excess.

3. CREATE EAR WIRES OR PURCHASE COPPER EAR WIRES

To make ear wires, cut a 6"–8" (15cm–20cm) piece of 20-gauge copper wire. Use round-nose pliers to make a small loop for connecting the earring. Use your fingers to form the ear wire shape and trim excess. Repeat Steps 1–3 for the other earring.

Chinatown

Our trip to San Francisco provided surprises around every corner. Each part of the city offered a new experience, and it wasn't until afterwards, looking through our photos, that I could take it all in. To this day, I am amazed by the diversity of the sights we saw in just one American city. I love this photo because it captures the hustle and bustle of Chinatown, a feeling I wanted to convey in this bracelet. The colors are bold and contrasting, yet somehow work together, much like the various cultures in this city.

MATERIALS

Bracelet

10 3mm white cubes

30 red glass chips

20 turquoise-colored chips

21 black seed beads

15½" (39cm) piece of memory wire

2¼" (6cm) black rubber tubing

Dangle

2 red glass chips

1 turquoise-colored chip

1 headpin

1 silver split ring

TOOLS

memory wire cutters

round-nose pliers

FINISHED LENGTH: 15" (38cm)

GET INSPIRED!

Do you have a shoebox full of photos that you haven't looked at in a while? Take some time to sift through them in search of color combinations and interesting shapes. Photos of crowds or city skylines provide great inspiration for eclectic mixtures of colors and textures.

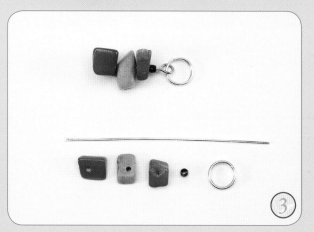

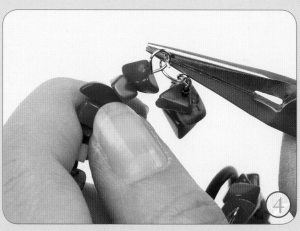

1. Begin pattern

Using memory wire cutters, cut a 16" (41cm) piece of memory wire. At one end, make a loop (see Making a Loop on page 13).

Add beads in the following pattern: five red chips, black seed bead, white cube, black seed bead, five turquoise chips, black seed bead, white cube, black seed bead, red/turquoise/red/turquoise/red chips, black seed bead, white cube, black seed bead, five turquoise chips, black seed bead, white cube, black seed bead, five red chips, black seed bead, white cube, black seed bead, 2¼" (6cm) piece of rubber tubing.

2. Finish bracelet

Repeat the pattern from Step 1 in reverse, beginning with the black seed bead and ending with the five red chips.

Use the round-nose pliers to make a final loop. Using the memory wire cutters, trim any excess wire.

3. Assemble dangle

On a headpin, add a red/turquoise/red chip and a black seed bead. Make a loop and trim excess wire. Add a split ring to the loop (see Connecting Split Rings on page 15).

4. Attach dangle

Using needle-nose pliers, attach the dangle to one of the loops at the end of the bracelet.

ᚑ Variation: Chinatown Earrings ᚑ

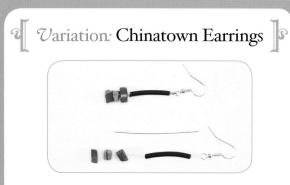

Earrings are always fun to make because they are quick and easy. In this case, the rubber tubing gives the earrings length and helps continue the eclectic "Chinatown" color theme.

MATERIALS

4 white seed beads
4 red glass chips
2 turquoise-colored chips
2" (5cm) black rubber tubing
2 2" (5cm) headpins
2 silver earwires

ASSEMBLE EARRINGS

On a silver headpin, add a red chip/turquoise chip/red chip, a white seed bead, a 1" (3cm) piece of black rubber tubing and a white seed bead. Make a loop and connect it to the ear wire.

Repeat for the second earring.

Moon and Stars Bracelet

I recently toured a planetarium—a great hands-on reminder of the wonders of space. As much as scientists and explorers have observed and discovered, there is so much more we still don't know. Aside from those rare moments of deep thought, most of the time I just enjoy the brightness of a full moon and the twinkle of the stars against the dark sky. This became sort of an arts and crafts project, which adds to the fun of interpreting real life into jewelry pieces. I stopped just short of getting out the glitter, but that doesn't mean you have to!

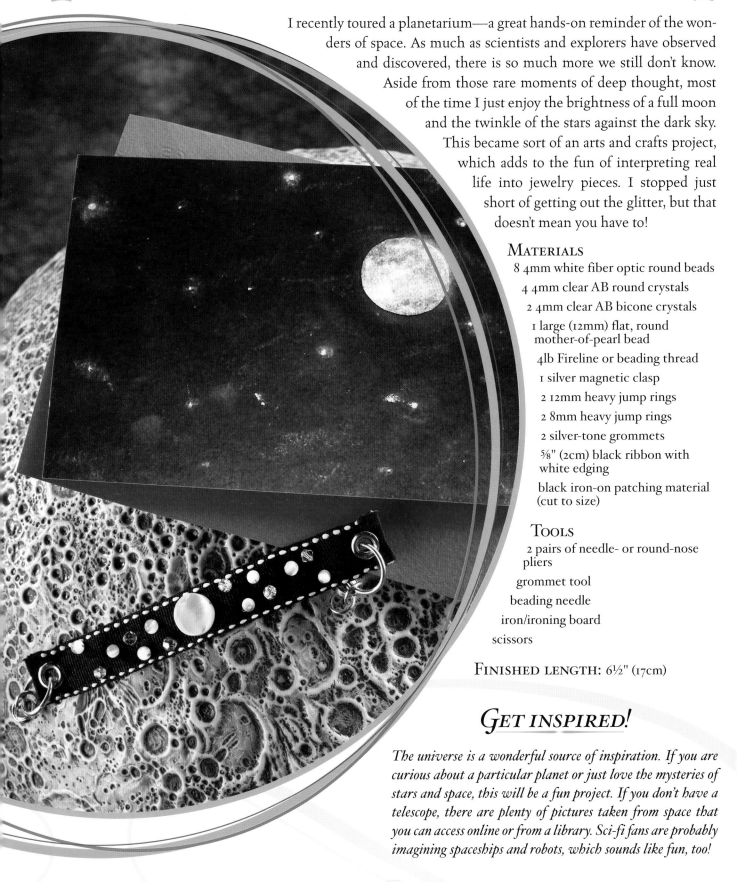

MATERIALS

8 4mm white fiber optic round beads

4 4mm clear AB round crystals

2 4mm clear AB bicone crystals

1 large (12mm) flat, round mother-of-pearl bead

4lb Fireline or beading thread

1 silver magnetic clasp

2 12mm heavy jump rings

2 8mm heavy jump rings

2 silver-tone grommets

⅝" (2cm) black ribbon with white edging

black iron-on patching material (cut to size)

TOOLS

2 pairs of needle- or round-nose pliers

grommet tool

beading needle

iron/ironing board

scissors

FINISHED LENGTH: 6½" (17cm)

GET INSPIRED!

The universe is a wonderful source of inspiration. If you are curious about a particular planet or just love the mysteries of stars and space, this will be a fun project. If you don't have a telescope, there are plenty of pictures taken from space that you can access online or from a library. Sci-fi fans are probably imagining spaceships and robots, which sounds like fun, too!

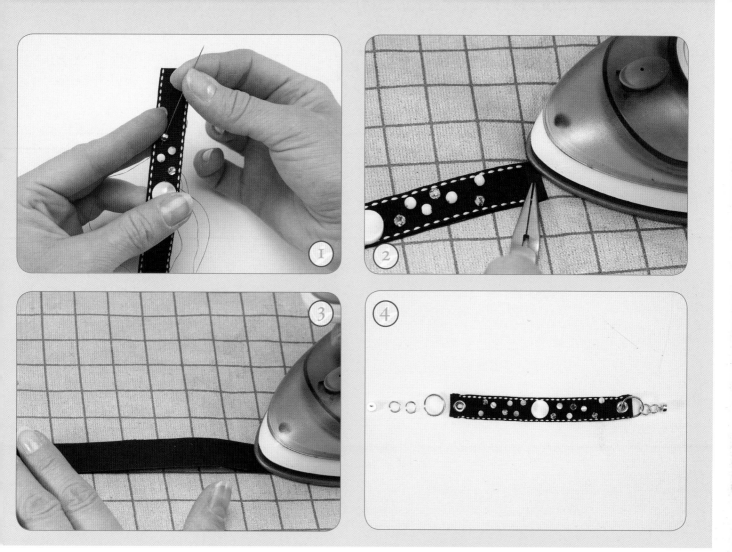

1. Sew on beads

Using the scissors, cut a 5" (13cm) piece of ribbon. Cut a piece of black iron-on material to 5½" (14cm). Thread the beading needle and make an overhand knot at the end of the thread (see Tying an Overhand Knot on page 12). Determine the center point on the ribbon and sew on the 12mm "moon" bead. To the left of the mother-of-pearl bead, sew on beads in a diagonal pattern: round crystal, two fiber optic beads, round crystal, two fiber optic beads and a bicone crystal. Leave space at the end for the grommet.

2. Iron patch

Repeat the mirror image of the pattern in Step 1 on the other side of the mother-of-pearl bead. On an ironing board, lay the iron-on material adhesive side up. Place the ribbon over the iron-on material so the overlay on each end is ¼" (6mm). Turn the overlay section to the front of the ribbon to cover the raw edge and hold it down with a pair of pliers. Run the point of the iron over the flap several times until the iron-on material adheres.

3. Iron backing

Repeat ironing the flap on the other side. Let the fabric cool. Turn the piece over. Using the hot iron, gently iron over the back of the ribbon several times until the iron-on material adheres.

4. Add clasp

Set aside to cool. Following the manufacturer's instructions for the grommet tool, attach the grommets to the ends of the ribbon just past the iron-on overlay. Use two pairs of round- or needle-nose pliers to connect a large jump ring to a small jump ring, and attach the large jump ring to the grommet (see Opening and Closing Jump Rings on page 15). Add a magnetic clasp to the small jump ring. Repeat on the other side.

Tip

If you have never used a grommet tool before, use a piece of scrap ribbon and iron-on material to experiment with the amount of pressure needed to secure the grommet.

Wrought Iron Fence

Crafting jewelry from photos encourages me to focus on details I would have only glanced at before. I decided to put this jewelry-making method to the test by randomly selecting an architectural detail, taking a photo, and creating a piece of jewelry. I took a few pictures of interesting scrollwork on an old home, an old-fashioned city drinking fountain and a wrought iron fence. I particularly liked the composition of the brick, trees and wrought iron.

Inspired, I went to the craft store, and when I found these circular beads, my idea became a reality. After a bit of sketching, as well as a little trial and error, I mimicked the structure of a wrought iron fence to create a wearable piece of art.

MATERIALS
7 grayish-blue circle beads
50 gunmetal gray bugle beads
12" (30cm) memory wire
20" (51cm) 26-gauge black craft wire
1 silver magnetic clasp
1 3-strand clasp connector
2 small silver jump rings

TOOLS
wire cutters
memory-wire cutters
round- or needle-nose pliers

FINISHED LENGTH: 7" (18cm)

GET INSPIRED!

Get your camera, take a walk and find some inspiration! Focus on the details of a house on your street, a nearby park or your favorite coffee shop—it will take your jewelry-design skills to a different level!

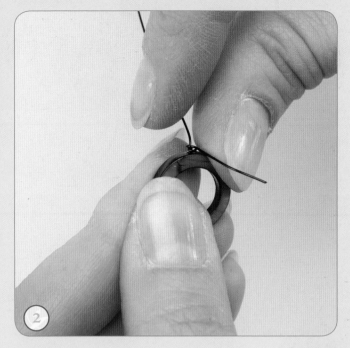

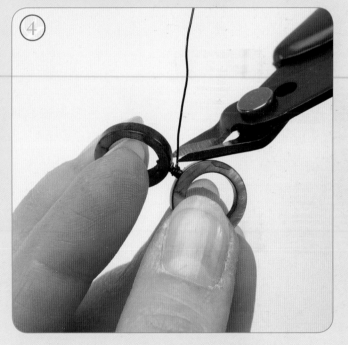

1. CUT WIRE

Using wire cutters, cut ten 2" (5cm) pieces of 26-gauge black craft wire. Run one 2" (5cm) piece of the black wire through a hole in a circular bead.

2. TWIST WIRE

Pull both ends of the wire together at the outside hole. Twist the wires twice.

3. ADD BEAD

Using the wire cutters, trim the short end of wire on the side of the bead where the wire shows on top. Add a circle bead to the remaining wire.

4. WRAP WIRE OVER SECOND BEAD

Pull the end of the wire to the side of the bead with the wire showing. Wrap the remaining wire two to three times over the wire between the two beads. Using the wire cutters, trim the excess wire.

5. ADD ADDITIONAL BEADS

Repeat Steps 1–4 until all seven circle beads are connected. Thread a 2" (5cm) piece of wire through one of the end beads. Make a wrapped loop that connects the end bead to the center hole of the clasp connector (see Making a Wire-Wrapped Loop on page 14). Using the wire cutters, trim any excess wire. Repeat for the other side of the clasp.

6. PREPARE MEMORY WIRE BANDS

Using the round-nose pliers, make a loop on one end of one of the pieces of memory wire. Add twenty-five bugle beads. Make a loop on the other end of the wire. Repeat for the second piece of wire.

7. COMPLETE BRACELET

Add a jump ring to each side of the magnetic clasp (see Opening and Closing Jump Rings on page 15). Add the magnetic clasp to the clasp connector using the jump rings.

   Using needle-nose pliers, connect the memory wire pieces to the corresponding outer hole on the clasp connector. Repeat for the final memory wire piece.

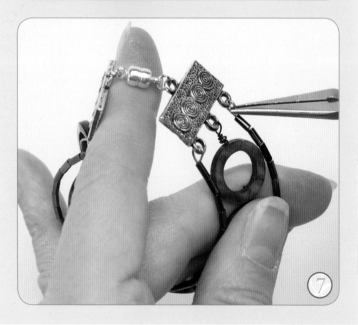

Frank Lloyd Wright

After I became a homeowner, I scoured decorating magazines for ideas. I didn't know what style I liked at the time, but I kept coming back to this Frank Lloyd Wright-inspired glass piece. It has been displayed in my home ever since, and I have never tired of the geometric design or colors. It took awhile to locate the ceramic beads and to come up with a method for framing the rows, but now I have a little piece of art that doesn't have to be displayed on a shelf.

MATERIALS

60 silver decorative tube beads

12 blue ceramic rectangular tube beads

12 turquoise ceramic rectangular tube beads

6 red ceramic rectangular tube beads

silver chain links

45" (114cm) .015 beading wire

10 silver-tone crimp tubes

2 silver heavy-duty magnetic clasps

TOOLS

wire cutters

FINISHED LENGTH:

7" (18cm)

GET INSPIRED!

Schedule a trip to a local museum, peruse online artwork or look through some of your own creations to find something that speaks to you. You will know what you like by paying attention to your feelings. When you feel inspired, break out the beads!

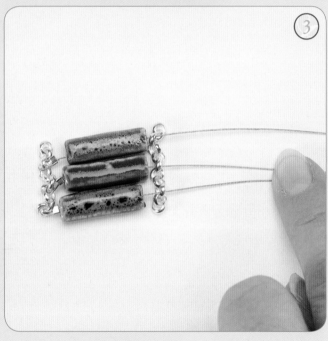

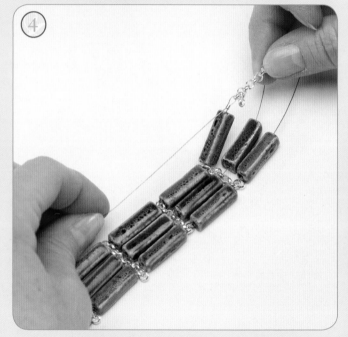

1. PREPARE CHAINS

Using wire cutters, cut seven pieces of chain to eleven links each.

2. ADD WIRE

Cut five 9" (23cm) strands of beading wire.

Attach three of the strands with a flattened crimp tube to chain links 3, 6 and 9 across (see Flattening Crimp Beads or Tubes on page 12). Trim any excess wire ends.

3. BEGIN ADDING BEADS

Thread on the beads in the following manner:

Top strand: turquoise bead

Middle strand: red bead

Bottom strand: blue bead

Add a length of chain so the respective wires are inserted into chain links 3, 6 and 9.

4. CONTINUE PATTERN

Repeat Step 3 until you have used all seven pieces of chain.

At the final piece of chain, add a crimp bead to secure the wire to the corresponding chain link.

5. Secure clasp

Chain links 1 and 11 across are beaded last and will each be attached to a separate clasp. Add a crimp bead to the end of one piece of wire and attach it to the magnetic clasp.

Run the wire through the end link on the chain spacer (either link 1 or 11).

6. Add outer beads

Add five silver tube beads. Run the wire through the next corresponding chain. Continue this pattern until reaching the final chain link.

7. Finish bracelet

Add a crimp tube and secure it to the corresponding link. Thread the wire through the last added bead to help hide the wire. Trim any excess wire.

Repeat Steps 5–7 on the other side of the bracelet.

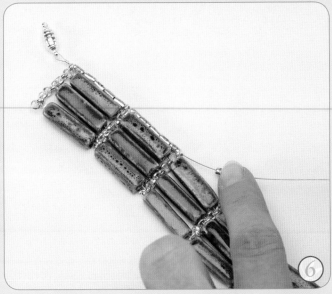

Geometric Wall Art

I didn't realize how fascinated I am with circles until I took a good look around my home. The inspiration for this piece is actually a pleather rug I use as a wall hanging. It's one of my favorite circular designs because it uses different variations of the same colors throughout.

This very simple design just requires opening and closing jump rings, and uses similar colors to the inspirational wall hanging. The challenge was how to represent the circle-inside-a-circle aspect. I used metal jump rings in lots of metallic colors to give it the right feel.

MATERIALS

large-hole glass pony beads in the following colors:

6 black

5 topaz

4 frosted topaz

4 frosted dark topaz

4 frosted light amber

3/8" jump rings in the following colors:

14 black

12 copper

12 bronze-tone

11 gold-tone

2 split rings

1 medium-sized toggle clasp

TOOLS

needle-nose pliers

2 pairs of needle- or round-nose pliers

electrical tape (optional)

FINISHED LENGTH: 18½" (47cm)

GET INSPIRED!

While sitting in a comfortable room in your house, look around at the design patterns in your artwork, knickknacks, fabrics and furniture. Are there any wave patterns, plaids, interesting graphics or color combinations that intrigue you? Can you interpret that into a piece of jewelry using beads, wire, fibers, etc.?

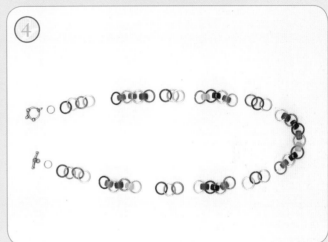

1. Create dangle sections

Create the pieces of the dangle as shown here (see Opening and Closing Jump Rings on page 15).

Connect a bronze and black jump ring.

Open a gold jump ring wide enough to slip on two black glass beads, one on either side of the notch in the ring. Close the ring.

Dangle three jump rings with beads from the gold jump ring in between the two black beads.

2. Add bottom three dangle pieces

Add the three beaded jump rings to the gold jump ring between the two black beads.

3. Add top dangle piece

Add the top dangle piece to the gold jump ring between the black beads.

4. Create sections

Create sections of the necklace by connecting the individual jump rings and adding beads as illustrated in Step 1. I began with a copper jump ring in the center and worked my way out on both sides, making sure both sides were even.

TIP

If necessary, use a little electrical or masking tape on the ends of the pliers to soften the surface and protect the jump rings.

5. CONNECT SECTIONS

Using two pairs of needle-nose pliers, connect the sections of the necklace.

6. CONNECT TOGGLE CLASP

Add the split ring and the toggle to the jump rings at each end of the necklace.

7. ATTACH DANGLE TO NECKLACE

Attach the dangle at the center copper jump ring of the necklace.

❧[Variation: Earrings]❧

This is a bold necklace that seemed to call out for a simple pair of matching earrings. Adding a matching pair of earrings is also a nice way to use any leftover beads.

MATERIALS
2 bronze-tone
flip-closure ear wires
2 bronze-tone
split rings
2 bronze-tone
jump rings
2 black jump rings
2 frosted light topaz
pony beads
2 frosted dark topaz
pony beads

ASSEMBLE EARRINGS
Connect jump rings,
beads and ear wires in the
combinations shown above

Colored Pencil Art

This necklace definitely falls under the category of wearable art! I colored this design years ago during my colored pencil phase and liked it so much that I framed it and hung it in my living room. Is it art? I suppose that is an individual opinion, but I think so and wondered if I could bring it to life in some three-dimensional way. When I came across this large black loop in the beading aisle, I knew I had stumbled upon my destiny and had to figure out how to wear this pencil design!

MATERIALS

16 6mm copper crystal round beads

19 6mm black faceted round beads

1 large black ring in matte finish

1 mini black ring in matte finish

1 natural shell ring

.014 midnight black fine beading wire

.014 autumn brown fine beading wire

1 bronze-tone clasp

5 bronze-tone crimp beads

TOOLS

needle-nose pliers

wire cutters

FINISHED NECKLACE LENGTH: 15" (38cm)

FINISHED PENDANT LENGTH: 2" (5cm)

GET INSPIRED!

Feel like doodling? Let your mind wander with pen and paper in your hand and see what you come up with. This is a fun experiment that might express your mood or your inner feelings. I have a tendency to draw interconnected circles and spirals. You are likely to come up with a beading pattern you never thought of before!

1. CREATE PENDANT

Cut two 36" (91cm) strands of midnight black wire. Stack the three focal rings in size order, with the small black ring on top. Loop both strands through all three of the focal pendant rings.

Add a black round bead over the two wire strands and slide it to the center of the rings. Bring all four strands together with the rings in the middle. String a crimp bead over all four wires and flatten to secure the pendant (see Flattening Crimp Beads and Tubes on page 12).

2. BEGIN WEAVE

Take two black strands to the left and two to the right. Starting with the left side, take the two strands on the left side and run each end through a black round bead from the opposite direction (the right strand through the bead from the right and the left strand through the bead from the left) to make a loop.

Take the two black wires through a copper round bead from opposite directions, then pull until the loop is evenly rounded. Make another loop adding a black round bead.

Repeat until you use nine black beads and eight copper beads.

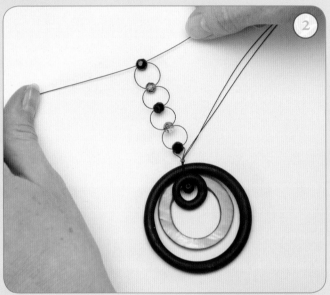

3. ADD COPPER WIRE

Cut two 34" (83cm) strands of autumn brown wire. Run one strand through the first black round bead closest to the pendant. Even out the ends so each side of the brown wire is the same length.

Run the ends of the wire through the second black round bead so it forms a loop around the two black loops. This will create a large brown loop with two inner black loops.

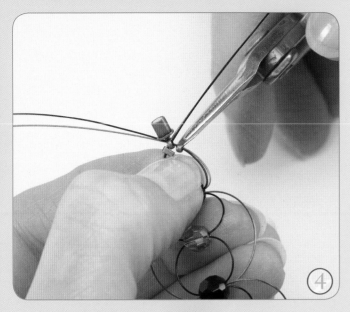

4. Add clasp

Continue looping in the black round beads until you reach the top black bead. A brown and a black wire will be coming out of the last bead added on each side. Place a crimp bead on each side over the two wires. Place the clasp on the left side wires after the crimp bead. Take the two wires on the left and slide them through the crimp bead on the right

Take the two wires on the right through the clasp and crimp bead on the left. Pull all of the loose wires gently to form a small loop with all wires going through the crimps and clasp.

Use the flat-nose pliers to flatten each of the crimp beads.

5. Trim excess wire

Using wire cutters, trim the excess wire on both sides of the clasp.

6. Finish necklace

Repeat Steps 3–5 for the right side of the necklace.

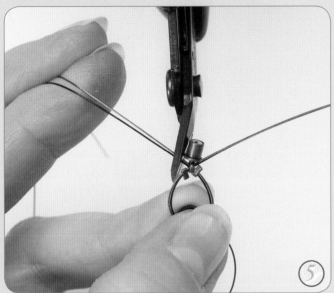

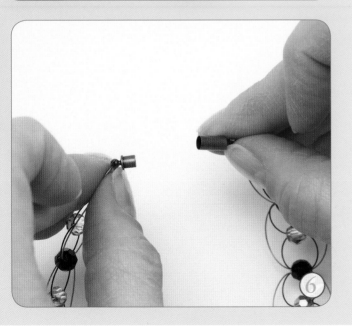

Chapter 2: Outdoor Ideas

Much human inspiration and invention comes from nature. As you study some of the wonderful gifts of the natural world, you might discover, as I did, that it really is important to slow down and literally smell the roses—or the dandelions!

The beads and components used in many of these projects were selected based on their similarity in color, shape or feeling to the inspirational objects from nature. When it comes to finding the "perfect" beads, it's also important to enjoy the treasure-hunting experience. It sometimes takes awhile, but it is usually worth it!

Finding the beads for the *Niagara Falls* multiple-strand bracelet (see page 46) was cause for celebration. It was important to find beads that were sparkly and could represent falling water. A simple stringing technique was all that was needed to bring this project to life.

Other projects inspired by nature, such as *Grand Cayman Island* (see page 48), *Rainbow Bracelet* (see page 51) and *End of Fall* (see page 66), involve a variety of stringing techniques. The *Dandelion* bracelet's band (see page 57) is simply two beaded strands that run through the yellow flower structure. It combines a bit of sewing and beading and clears the way for endless other color combinations.

Several of these projects, such as *Florida Palms* (see page 54) and *Strawflower Cactus* (see page 60), incorporate techniques created during the design phase that were new to me. They allowed me to bring my ideas to fruition and included a few happy accidents along the way.

[Niagara Falls]

Niagara Falls in Ontario, Canada, is a beautiful place to visit. My parents, husband and I enjoyed taking the bus tour for a day through all the sights. We went behind the Falls and on the *Maid of the Mist*. In this photo, a hot air balloon is passing over the American side of the Falls. To remember this trip, I wanted the most literal interpretation of the Falls possible. I was thrilled to find these bugle beads: When they are massed together, they almost look like moving water. Finding these beads gave me a great sense of accomplishment. I didn't realize how much fun it would be to make jewelry like this.

MATERIALS
194 ceylon beads
248 white bugle beads
58 4mm AB bicone crystals
60 silver-lined seed beads
.12 fine or very flexible beading wire
28 small silver crimp tubes
1 4-strand silver bar clasp

TOOLS
wire cutters
needle-nose pliers
round-nose pliers

FINISHED LENGTH: 6½" (17cm)

GET INSPIRED!

Looking through old photos allows us to re-create past experiences in our memory and can even bring the feelings associated with them to the surface. Why not use that ability to your advantage to increase your overall happiness quotient? Once you identify an experience that brought you great joy or excitement, you might be surprised to find you are continually remembering things about it as you create your piece. The extra serotonin created is just icing on the cake!

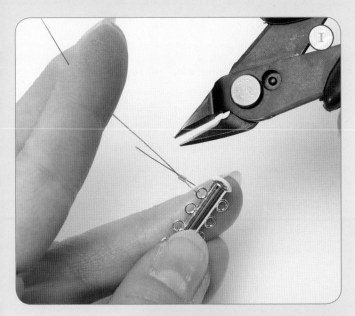

1. PREPARE WIRE
Using wire cutters, cut fourteen 9" (23cm) strands of beading wire. Begin by attaching one wire on an outer loop of the clasp using a crimp tube (see Flattening Crimp Tubes on page 12).

TIP

Flattening the small crimp tubes will simplify this multistrand project

2. BEGIN STRINGING
Begin stringing full strands of beads, with three strands to each outer loop and four to each inner loop of the clasp, in the following manner:

> Outside loops: two strands of ninety-seven ceylon beads each; one strand of alternating silver-lined seed beads and 4mm bicone crystals (thirty seed beads and twenty-nine bicone crystals).

> Eight inner strands: thirty-one bugle beads each

Attach each strand to the corresponding one on the opposite clasp end by following Step 1.

3. BEGIN COIL
Using wire cutters, cut a 2' (1m) piece of 24-gauge wire. Hold the memory wire strands approximately ¾" (2cm) apart. Center the 24-gauge wire to the memory wire. Wrap one side of the wire around the memory wire to secure it. Repeat for the other side.

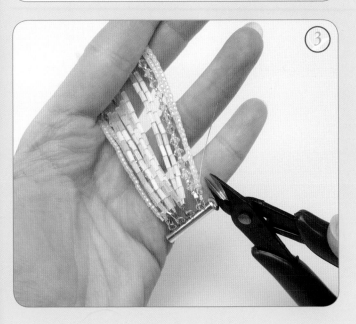

〖Variation: Niagara Falls Earrings〗

I wanted to make a pair of earrings with sparkle to accompany the Niagara Falls bracelet. I also wanted to continue with the "running water" theme. It wasn't until I finished them using the crystal AB rounds that I realized they resembled the hot air balloon hovering over the American Falls.

MATERIALS
2 8mm AB crystal round beads
40 9/0 white ceylon beads
16 white ridged bugle beads
8 silver headpins
2 silver eyepins
2 silver ear wires

1. PREPARE PIECES
Add beads to headpins as follows:
> Two headpins: ten white ceylon beads each
> Two headpins: four white bugle beads each.

Finish each headpin with a loop.

2. ASSEMBLE EARRINGS
Connect the eyepin to the ear wire. Slide on the 8mm crystal beads and finish with a loop. Attach the two ceylon bead headpins and two bugle bead headpins to the loop.

Repeat Steps 1 and 2 for the other earring.

Grand Cayman Island

I love the sun and the beach, so the tropical vacations we have taken are extra-special to me. Just looking at this photo brings a feeling of warmth and joy. For this project, matching the colors of the sand and sea was my priority. I was thrilled when I came across these tan and turquoise beads in a local bead shop. This jewelry will forever remind me of the beautiful setting on Grand Cayman's seven-mile beach.

MATERIALS

46 gold seed beads

27 4mm light aqua bicone crystals

47 4mm × 6mm tan mother-of-pearl beads

26 5mm × 5mm green turquoise Czech glass pinched beads

.12 gold-tone beading wire

gold tone lobster claw clasp

2 gold split rings

2 gold-tone ear wires

9 gold-tone headpins

3 gold-tone eyepins

2 gold-tone crimp beads or tubes

TOOLS

wire cutters

round-nose pliers

crimping tool or needle-nose pliers

FINISHED LENGTH: 7" (18cm)

GET INSPIRED!

The next time you drive down a highway, take a good look at the horizon. The morning sky offers a nice variety of layered colors to inspire beautiful jewelry pieces. At times, it has varying shades of red and pink that meet the dark earth and coordinate perfectly.

1. Prepare wire

Cut three 9" (23cm) strands of wire. Place a crimp bead over all three wires. Run the wires through the lobster claw clasp and either crimp or flatten to secure (see Using Crimp Beads or Tubes on page 12).

2. Add beads

String beads as follows:

> Strands 1 and 3: Alternate gold seed beads and tan beads using twenty-two tan beads and twenty-three gold seed beads on each strand.

> Strand 2: Alternate light aqua bicone crystals and green turquoise beads using seventeen green turquoise beads and eighteen light aqua bicone crystals.

3. Secure ends

Place a crimp bead over each strand. Run the wires through the gold split ring. Thread the wires back through at least one bead and crimp or flatten. Trim any excess wire.

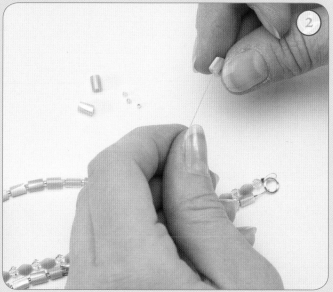

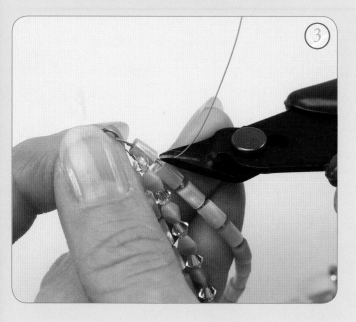

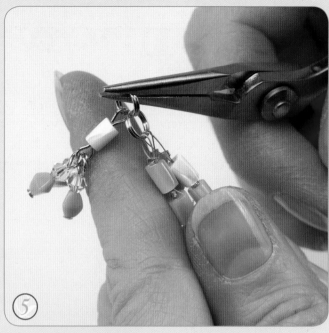

④

⑤

4. Make dangle components

On three headpins, add a green turquoise bead and a light aqua bicone crystal. Make a loop and trim the wire. On an eyepin, add one tan bead, make a loop and trim the wire. Attach the three beaded headpins to one end of the beaded eyepin. Attach a split ring to the top of the beaded eyepin. Connect this split ring to the split ring on the end of the bracelet to form the dangle.

5. Add dangle

Attach the dangle to the bracelet (see Connecting Split Rings on page 15).

Variation: Grand Cayman Island Earrings

These coordinating earrings are identical to the bracelet dangle above except they are connected to ear wires instead of a split ring.

Materials

2 4mm × 6mm tan mother-of-pearl beads
6 4mm light aqua bicone crystals
6 5mm × 5mm green turquoise Czech glass pinched beads
2 gold-tone ear wires
6 gold-tone headpins
1 gold-tone eyepins

Assemble earrings

Follow the bracelet dangle instructions in Step 4. Connect the ear wires to the top of the beaded eyepin in place of the split rings.

Rainbow Bracelet

Rainbows seem magical to me, but science tells us they are simply light rays hitting the water and refracting to produce a color based on their wavelength. You will typically see each of the seven colors you learned in school: red, orange, yellow, green, indigo and violet. It's amazing that rainbows are captured in photos, considering they are often fleeting. When you are in the vicinity of a waterfall, it's almost a given that you will see a rainbow whenever the sun shines. I wonder if a pot of gold is buried in the rocks somewhere. This bracelet represents this magical and often elusive gift of nature.

MATERIALS

49 6mm crystals in the following colors:

    7 red
    7 orange
    7 yellow (jonquil)
    7 green
    7 blue
    7 indigo (capri)
    7 violet

sky blue nylon-coated beading wire

2 crimp tubes with attached ring

1 silver-tone magnetic clasp

TOOLS

needle-nose pliers

wire cutters

masking tape

FINISHED LENGTH: 7" (18cm)

GET INSPIRED!

There are many awe-inspiring sights in the sky, such as clouds lit with golden rays of sunshine at dawn. As many beaders are probably aware, there is one sight that is so beautiful, a bead coating was created to mimic its multicolored effect. The aurora borealis is only visible in certain parts of the world, but there are many photos available for reference.

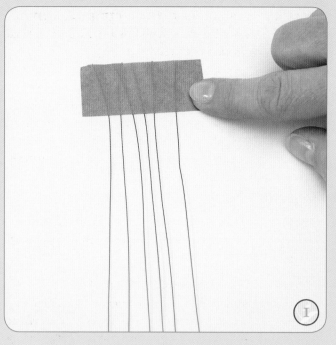

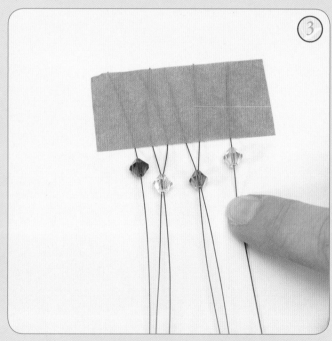

1. Prepare wire

Cut six 8½" (22cm) strands of sky blue beading wire.
Place strands with the ends evenly spaced on the
work surface. Secure the tops of the strands with
masking tape.

2. Begin bead pattern

Beginning at the left, thread a red crystal onto strand 1.
Thread a yellow crystal onto both strands 2 and 3.

3. Finish first row

Thread a blue crystal onto both strands 4 and 5.
Thread a violet crystal onto strand 6.

4. Continue pattern

Starting back at the left, thread an orange crystal onto
strands 1 and 2. Thread a green crystal onto both strands 3
and 4. Thread an indigo crystal onto both strands 5 and 6.

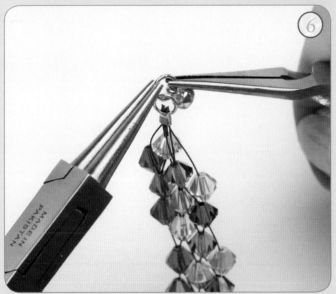

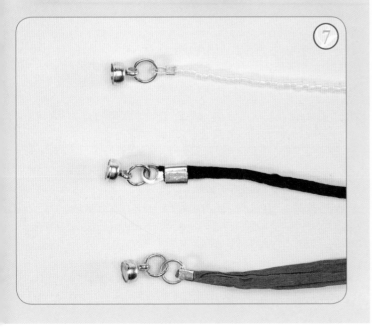

5. FINISH BRACELET AND SECURE STRANDS

Repeat the bead pattern in photos 2–4 until seven beads in each color have been used. Using a piece of tape, secure the bottoms of the threads to the work surface.

At the tops of the threads, carefully remove the tape and gather all six ends. Run the threads through a crimp tube. Ensure that the beads are evenly spaced and the wires are straight. Gently flatten the crimp tube with needle-nose pliers (see Flattening Crimp Tubes on page 12). Trim any excess wire.

6. ADD CLASP

Remove the tape holding down the other end and repeat the last part of Step 6. Add a jump ring and magnetic clasp to each end.

7. MAKE NECK CORD (OPTIONAL)

You can turn this bracelet into a choker by making a neck cord. There are many material options for making a neck cord, such as a strand of seed beads, silk cording and paper raffia (from top to bottom).

Florida Palms

During a winter snowfall in Ohio, I was pining for sunny Florida and the lovely palm trees blowing in the breeze. I remember thinking, "If I had a palm tree in my front yard, I would hug it every day!" I went through some photos from a stop-over in Hollywood, Florida, and, remembering the beauty of the palms, started feeling more cheerful.

I settled on working with hemp cord and macramé knots to mimic the palm trees and to give the piece a natural, textural feel. The beads and crystals were added for a little sunny sparkle.

MATERIALS

35–40 6/0 metallic green iris Czech glass E beads

35–40 4mm chrysolite green Swarovski crystals

5 palm wood beads

1mm–2mm green hemp cord

1 silver-tone lobster claw clasp

2 medium-sized split rings

Fireline or embroidery thread

TOOLS

scissors or cutting tool

beading needle

bead reamer

masking tape

push pin

FINISHED LENGTH: 7" (18cm)

GET INSPIRED!

Palm trees make me feel happy and peaceful, most likely because they are associated with sunshine and beaches! For some, that feeling might be associated with a pine tree in the middle of a forest. For others, a weeping willow tree leaning peacefully over a pond in summer may conjure up fond memories. Challenge yourself to create a piece of jewelry that translates that feeling.

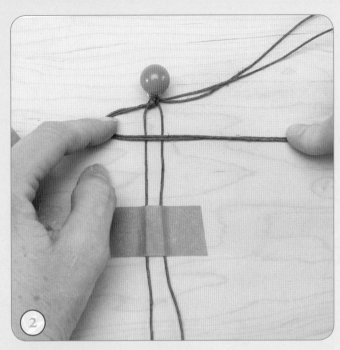

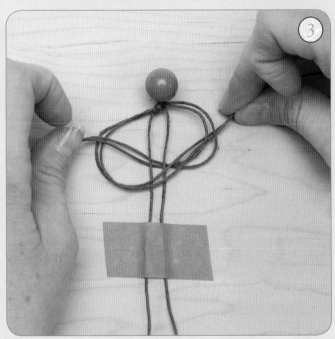

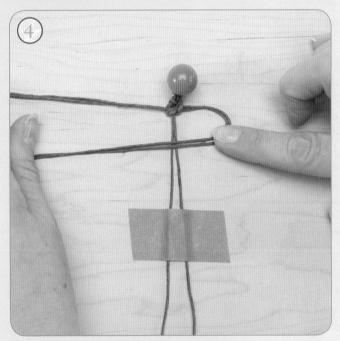

1. PREPARE CORDING

Cut two 6' (2m) pieces and one 7' (2m) piece of hemp cord. Pull all three strands through a split ring and bring the ends together. Make a single overhand knot to tie all the cords together at the split ring (see Tying an Overhand Knot on page 12).

2. BEGIN SQUARE KNOT

Using the push pin, secure the split ring to the work surface. Separate the six strands by pulling two 3' (91cm) strands to the left, and two to the right. Using the masking tape, secure the two 3½' (107cm) strands to the work surface in the middle. Make the first half of a square knot by placing the two left strands over the inner strands.

3. CONTINUE SQUARE KNOT

Bring the two right strands under the inner strands and up through the loop made by the left strands.

4. REPEAT BEGINNING WITH RIGHT STRANDS

Pull the left and right double strands with even pressure until the knot rests firmly at the initial overhand knot. The second part of the square knot is made the same way, but starts on the right side.

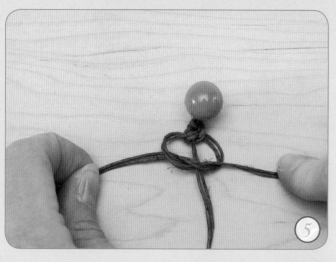

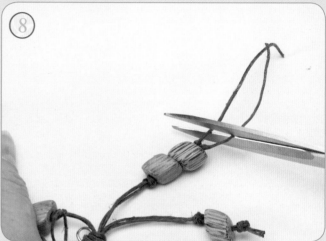

5. FINISH SQUARE KNOT

Pull the left and right double strands with even pressure until the knot rests firmly against the first part of the square knot.

*T*IP

Use a bead reamer to enlarge the palm wood bead holes as needed.

6. CREATE BOW

Remove the tape from the inner strands and make a bow using just those two strands. Pull the two loops until they are even.

7. ADD BEADS

Smooth the loops, place a finger on the knot, pull both strands downward and re-tape them to the work surface. Continue this pattern until it reaches the desired length.

Thread the beading needle with Fireline or embroidery thread. Make an overhand knot at the end of the thread and take the needle up through the first square knot. Sew on the beads, alternating between the crystals and E beads.

8. FINISH BRACELET

Alternate sewing E beads and crystals along the full length of the bracelet. Make a few knots with the needle and thread to secure the beads when finished.

Place the lobster claw clasp on the split ring. Pull all six strands through the split ring. Tie an overhand knot.

Make the dangles by placing one or two palm wood beads over each pair of strands. Knot the strands near the ends and trim. Secure the knot with glue if needed.

Dandelion

This bracelet is my ode to the dandelion. The yellow is as bright as the sun and contrasts beautifully with the bright green spring grass. I have childhood memories of playing with dandelions and treating them like flowers. It was only after moving to the suburbs that I discovered the poor little dandelion had lost its respect. If you can't have a dandelion in your yard for fear of populating the entire neighborhood with "weeds," then wearing one on your wrist is the next best thing!

MATERIALS

8–10g 8/0 opaque yellow seed beads

5g 11/0 opaque yellow luster beads

4lb test .20mm clear fine fishing line

.012 bead stringing wire

4 2" (5cm) pieces neon green rubber memory wire tubing

1 brooch form with round pin

4 gold-tone crimp tubes

1 gold-tone magnetic clasp

TOOLS

beading needle

wire cutters

crimping tool

round-nose pliers

needle-nose pliers

FINISHED LENGTH:
7½" (18cm)

GET INSPIRED!

Are there simple things in nature that you find appealing? You can visit a park or natural setting to see an old-fashioned clover, dandelion, violet or miscellaneous volunteer flower growing among some nice green grass. If you have time for a nature walk, look for simple forgotten "weeds" to use for inspiration.

1. SECURE WIRE

Use needle-nose pliers to gently pull the pin off the back cover of the brooch form.

Thread the beading needle with 3' (91cm) of clear fishing line. Tie an overhand knot at the end of the line (see Tying an Overhand Knot on page 12). Add an 11/0 bead. Take the needle up through the center of the brooch form.

Take the needle back down through the brooch form from another hole and back up through the bead underneath to secure the line.

TIP

You may have to sand the back of the pin plate after removing the pin clasp.

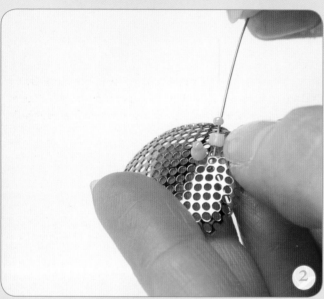

2. ADD BEADS

With the needle on the topside of the form, place an 8/0 and 11/0 bead on the line.

Take the needle over the 11/0 bead and through the 8/0 bead and back through the same hole in the form. Bring the needle back up through the hole next to the one just completed and repeat the process.

3. FILL FORM

Continue until the form is covered. Take the needle to the underside of the form and add an 8/0 bead. Tie a knot around the bead and take it back up and down through the form and knot a final time.

TIP

If there are any gaps, go back and fill them before completing Step 4. Some spots on the form will need to have two sets of beads attached to fill any gaps.

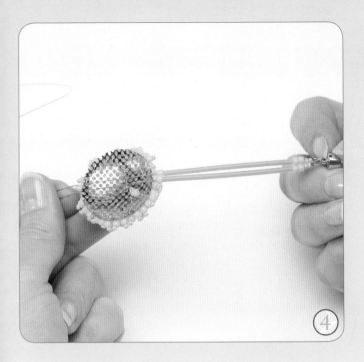

4. ADD BRACELET SIDES

Add a dot of glue or just trim the line leaving approximately ¼" (3mm), which will be covered by the back of the brooch form.

Cut two 10" (25cm) strands of wire. String a 8/0 bead, a 2" (5cm) piece of rubber tubing, two 8/0 beads and two 11/0 beads. Add the crimp bead to each strand and use the crimping tool to finish. Run the wire through two side-by-side holes in the top edge of the form, underneath the form and then back up through two side-by-side holes in a similar position on the other side of the form.

To each strand add an 8/0 bead, a 2" (5cm) piece of rubber tubing, two 8/0 beads and two 11/0 beads. Use a crimp bead to secure (see using Crimp Beads and Tubes on page 12).

5. FINISH BRACELET

Trim any excess wire. Using needle-nose pliers, turn the prongs on the back side of the form so they are pointing at a 45° angle or lower. Reassemble the form and secure the prongs.

TIP

Keep an eye on the underside of the form so the line doesn't get tangled or caught on the form's edge.

Variation: Dandelion Earrings

This bracelet was just calling out for earrings—especially because each earring looks like an individual representation of the sweet yellow dandelion!

MATERIALS
2 8mm yellow glass round beads
2 8/0 opaque yellow seed beads
2 ¼" (6mm) pieces neon green rubber memory wire tubing
2 gold-tone headpins
2 gold-tone ear wires

ASSEMBLE EARRINGS
Add beads to your headpin as follows: 8mm yellow round bead, 8/0 seed bead, rubber tubing. Make a loop (see Making a Loop on page 13) and trim any excess wire.

Connect the loop to the ear wire. Repeat for the other earring.

Strawflower Cactus

The strawflower cactus appears to have paper flowers attached to it. I have several of these plants in a variety of colors, including neon green, neon yellow, fuchsia and this coppery yellow. When you take the time to study plants and flowers closely, you will never be disappointed. I wanted to find beads to represent the way the flower sits above the cactus points. As you change your perspective and make jewelry to represent actual objects, you will likely create new ways to integrate beads and materials to achieve the desired outcome. Here, I used an unusual technique to keep the bicones sitting on top of the cactus beads.

MATERIALS

Bracelet

46 green drop beads

24 topaz glass bicones

9½" (24cm) memory wire

18" (46cm) 4–8lb test clear monofilament stringing line

Dangle

2 4mm topaz glass bicones

2 6mm topaz glass bicones

1 silver-tone headpin

1 silver-tone split ring

TOOLS

beading needle

memory wire cutting tool

round- or flat-nose pliers

FINISHED LENGTH: 9" (23cm)

GET INSPIRED!

All flowers are intricate creations, but some seem to defy logic with their unusual behaviors or appearances. Take a stroll through your local nursery and look for an unusual creation. Did you find something that made you scratch your head in wonderment or make you laugh? Re-create it in a piece of jewelry and share that experience with others as you wear it!

TIP

Use glass bicones rather than crystals in this design so they won't cut the clear line.

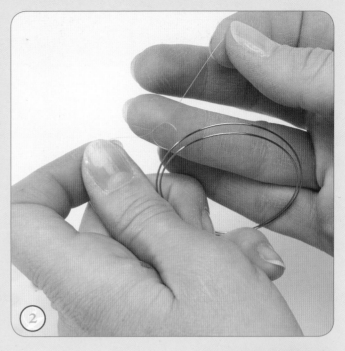

I. STRING ON BEADS

Thread the needle with monofilament stringing line and knot the end. String on a pattern of two drop beads and one bicone until you have used all the beads.

2. SECURE LINE TO MEMORY WIRE

Make a loop on one end of the memory wire (see Making a Loop on page 13). Remove the needle from the line and double-knot the line to the memory wire at the midpoint.

3. THREAD BEADS ONTO MEMORY WIRE

Add the first two green drop beads to the memory wire, making sure to skip the bicone. (The bicones will not be strung on the memory wire.)

4. CONTINUE ADDING DROP BEADS

Continue stringing the green drop beads two at a time onto the memory wire. Begin gently moving the beads toward the looped end of the memory wire as you add beads.

5. Finish stringing

After stringing on the green drop beads, place the bicones above the drops. Starting from the looped end of the memory wire, adjust bead placement by gently pushing the drop beads together and, if necessary, take up slack from the clear line a section at a time.

Make the final memory wire loop and trim off any excess wire. Knot the end of the clear line just above the new loop. Add a drop of glue if needed.

6. Create dangle

String the following onto a headpin: one 4mm topaz bicone, two 6mm topaz bicones and one 4mm topaz bicone.

7. Attach dangle

Make a loop and trim any excess wire.

Add a split ring to one of the looped ends of the memory wire (see Connecting Split Rings on page 15). Attach the dangle to the split ring.

Spring Blossoms

Have you ever driven down a street lined with cherry blossom trees in full bloom? These gorgeous trees seem to bloom overnight. They help to erase all memories of blizzards and ice storms and bring expectations of greenery and flowers. When I looked at these trees closely, I discovered that the contrast between the white flowers and the dark tree limbs and trunk is what makes the flowers stand out so beautifully. This bracelet is simple and fun to make. As with the cherry blossom trees, the dark wire "branches" make the rainbow beads stand out in this design.

MATERIALS
24g 6/o crystal AB beads
1 black E bead
24-gauge black craft wire
1 silver-tone lobster claw clasp
1 silver-tone split ring

TOOLS
wire cutters
needle- or round-nose pliers

FINISHED LENGTH: 7½"
(19cm)

GET INSPIRED!

Spring is such a fresh and welcoming time. As each day passes, people discard their heavy coats and become a little more active. Birds become noticeably more chipper and tulip bulbs begin to sprout. What is your favorite part about this time of year? Think about how you can express that by creating something fresh, new and maybe even different.

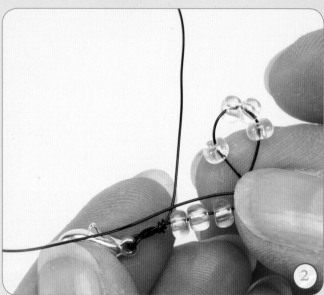

1. PREPARE WIRE

Using wire cutters, cut two 3' (1m) lengths of black wire. Run the two ends through the lobster claw clasp and twist the ends around the wires twice. Using the wire cutters, trim any excess wire.

Separate the wires. On one of the strands, add eight crystal beads.

2. CREATE LOOP

Using your fingers, slide the last four beads over to the clasp. Bring the long end of the wire around to form a loop with the four beads on it.

3. TWIST LOOP

Using your fingers, twist the loop with the beads on it to resemble a tree branch.

4. ADD BEADS TO OTHER WIRE

Repeat Steps 2–4 on the other piece of metal wire.

5. TWIST BRANCHES TOGETHER

Holding the branches with your fingers, twist the unlooped strands of beads together.

6. SHAPE BRANCHES

Using your fingers, press the branch loops down.

7. FINISH BRACELET

Repeat Steps 2–6 until you have reached the desired length. Using your fingers, shape the branches as you see fit. When you are finished, run the wires through the split ring. Make a wrapped loop (see Making a Wire-Wrapped Loop on page 14). Using the wire cutters, trim any excess wire.

End of Fall

If you spend most of your time indoors, you're missing out on millions of great photo opportunities provided by nature. This photo was taken between fall and winter. The green leaves had fallen from this tree, and the berries had turned bright red. I had never noticed the beauty of brown and red before and thought the starkness of the bare branches provided a great canvass for a bright color. I searched for the right combination of beads for this project and thought these "sticks" were a great find. Treasure hunting success!

MATERIALS

14 gold-tone top-drilled stick beads

24 5mm red glass beads

nylon-coated gold beading wire

1 gold- or bronze-tone toggle clasp

2 gold-tone crimp beads

TOOLS

wire cutters

needle-nose pliers or crimping tool

FINISHED LENGTH:

7¼" (18cm)

GET INSPIRED!

With camera in hand, step out your back door and get up-close to nature. Try zooming into your subject. From this perspective, you will likely find some great patterns and color contrasts you hadn't noticed before. Look at flowers, tree bark, decorative grasses, tree branches, fence posts holding up vines and vegetable gardens. You will be amazed at the number of things that will work perfectly as jewelry pieces.

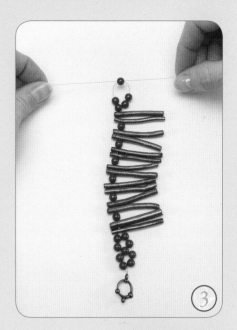

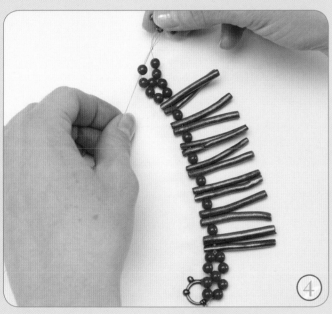

1. BEGIN BRACELET

Using the wire cutters, cut 19" (48cm) of beading wire. Place the toggle clasp on the wire and bring the two ends together. Add a crimp bead and flatten it to secure the toggle clasp (see Flattening Crimp Tubes on page 12).

On each side of the wire, string two red beads. On the left strand, add a third red bead. Thread the right strand through the third bead on the left strand. Pull both sides of wire to make a circle.

2. ADD STICK BEADS

String two stick beads over both strands.

3. FINISH PATTERN

Continue stringing beads on both strands in the following pattern: one red bead, two stick beads. Do this until

you reach the last two stick beads. After the last two stick beads, add three red beads on the left strand and two red beads on the right. Take the right strand through the third red bead on the left strand. Pull both sides of wire to make a circle.

4. ADD OTHER SIDE OF TOGGLE

Add two red beads on each strand. Add a crimp bead over both strands, and add the toggle clasp to the wires. Loop the wires so they pass through the crimp bead and down through the top red bead.

5. FINISH BRACELET

Pull the wire to tighten it around the toggle clasp. Crimp the crimp bead (see Using Crimp Beads or Tubes on page 12). Using the wire cutters, trim any excess wire.

Autumn Leaves

As the seasons transition from summer to fall, even those who never want summer to end cannot help but be awed by the glorious change in colors. Many people even plan trips to the country so they can commune with nature and appreciate the wonder of it all. My own backyard reflects this wonder as the trees fill with leaves in various shades of brown and yellow. I wanted to capture this free-falling, natural experience, and I discovered that random wire twisting was a fun way to do it.

MATERIALS

1 30mm × 24mm smoke-colored faceted leaf

1 30mm × 24mm honey-colored faceted leaf

20 6/0 or E beads in the following colors:

    4 copper

    4 gold

    4 frosted honey

    4 creamy brown

    4 transparent brown

6 4mm bronze bicones

24-gauge gold-tone craft wire

16" (41cm) necklace chain with clasp

2 gold-tone jump rings

TOOLS

needle-nose pliers

wire cutters

FINISHED CHAIN LENGTH:
16" (41cm)

FINISHED PENDANT LENGTH:
3" (8cm)

GET INSPIRED!

The gorgeous colors of autumn work in perfect harmony with each other and their surroundings. The combinations of red, gold, brown, yellow and green in varying shades are warm, inviting and balanced. If you are not sure which beads to put together, bead stores make different shades of bead mixes to meet every need. Try your hand at mixing your own or use a pre-mixed package to create a piece in warm, earthy tones.

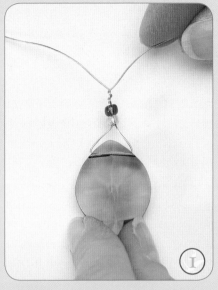

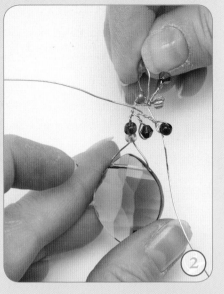

1. BEGIN PENDANT

Using the wire cutters, cut a 3' (1m) piece of wire. Run the wire through the smoke-colored faceted leaf and even out the ends. At the top of the leaf bead, pinch the two wires together to form a triangle. Add two 6/0 beads over both wires. Twist the wires together twice. Separate the wires.

2. BEGIN TWISTS

Add an E bead to one strand of wire. Hold the bead away from the pendant about ¼" (6mm) with one hand and bend the strand over at that point. With your other hand, hold the wire where it meets the pendant and make two or three twists with the bead.

Continue to add beads and twist in this manner until there are six to eight twists. Use your fingers to adjust for placement as needed.

3. ADD SECOND PENDANT

Repeat Steps 1 and 2 using the honey-colored leaf bead on the remaining wire.

4. CONTINUE TWISTS

When you have the desired amount of beads on the second strand, twist the wires together.

5. FINISH TWISTS

Using the wire cutters, trim off the shorter piece of wire. Continue adding and twisting beads to the longer piece of wire as desired. String the remaining wire through a jump ring and add two beaded twists that will hang down from the ring. Using the wire cutters, trim any excess wire.

6. ADD CHAIN

Determine the center point of the chain and add a jump ring to that link (see Opening and Closing Jump Rings on page 15). Attach the jump ring on the pendant to the jump ring on the chain.

Icicles

As a child, I was fascinated by icicles. I always had a strong urge to pull them off things, especially the giant ones. Sparkly icicles are often used in scenes to depict a fantasy-like winter wonderland. After one winter storm—once the roads were cleared and the sun came out—we were finally able to get out of the house. Walking through the neighborhood seemed surreal with mountains of snow everywhere and an eerie silence. It truly was a real-life winter wonderland. This pendant represents icicles hanging under a snowdrift and glistening in the sunshine—a nice reminder to embrace the beauty of what nature brings.

MATERIALS

1 white frosted glass bead

14 clear AB dagger beads

16" (41cm) silver-plated neck chain

3" (8cm) additional silver-plated neck chain

1 silver-plated necklace bail

1 silver eyepin

14 6mm silver-plated jump rings

TOOLS

2 pairs needle-nose pliers

round-nose pliers

wire cutters

FINISHED CHAIN LENGTH: 18" (46cm)

FINISHED PENDANT LENGTH: 3½" (9cm)

GET INSPIRED!

Can you see the beauty of all things in your surroundings? Can you see past the snowstorm that makes travel difficult and appreciate the crystal sparkles? Can you see past the rusty metal watering can that needs a coat of paint and appreciate its rustic beauty? Can you see past a fallen tree and appreciate that it will feed the earth beneath it? Be on the lookout for things that can provide you with an original perspective on beauty to express your creativity.

1. Connect chain and eyepin
Connect the 3" (8cm) piece of chain to the eyepin.

2. Add daggers
Place the white glass bead on the eyepin, and make a loop (see Making a Loop on page 13) with the round-nose pliers. Using the wire cutters, trim any excess wire.

Using two pairs of needle-nose pliers, add a dagger bead to a jump ring and attach it to the first chain link hanging from the white bead. The dagger bead will hang to either the left or right of the chain. Skip a chain link and add the next dagger bead on the opposite side as the first. Continue adding dagger beads on jump rings in this manner until the last dagger bead is hanging on the last chain link.

3. Add chain
Attach the necklace bail to the eyepin loop.
Open the neck chain and slide the end of the clasp through the bail.

Throughout life's journey, there are many things that bring us pleasure. I live in a climate that changes with the seasons, so it seems I spend quite a lot of time pining for warm weather and sandy beaches. Pieces that are inspired by these things serve as meaningful reminders of previous experiences, as well as anticipation of more to come.

Sometimes these experiences are fleeting and occur once in a lifetime. I would classify Hug a Dolphin (see page 86) as one of those experiences. I wanted to create something summery that clearly represented dolphins without using actual dolphin beads.

Other experiences are available to us on a daily basis in the form of yummy treats, like Box of Chocolates (see page 96), or comforting companions, as in Furry Family Members (see page 89). The projects in this chapter are based on elements in my life that bring me pleasure.

I hope you enjoy the techniques used in this chapter as much as I did—they stretched my imagination. When you begin working on projects to represent your life's pleasures, I know you will want to create new and interesting techniques, too. That's just an added pleasure!

The Sun

Sunshine always makes me feel happy. There is definitely a connection between weather and emotions! Since we can't count on seeing the sun every day, I made a representation of its warm glow. I have always admired jewelry designers who incorporate a sense of humor or silliness into their pieces, and I think I may have achieved that in this design.

MATERIALS

4 large yellow shell beads with ¼" (6mm) holes

140 translucent yellow seed beads

9 4mm light yellow faceted round beads

8½" (22cm) memory wire

24-gauge gold-tone craft wire

5 gold-tone jump rings

2 gold-tone ear wires

2 gold-tone eyepins

TOOLS

memory wire cutters

round- or needle-nose pliers

FINISHED LENGTH:
7¾" (20cm)

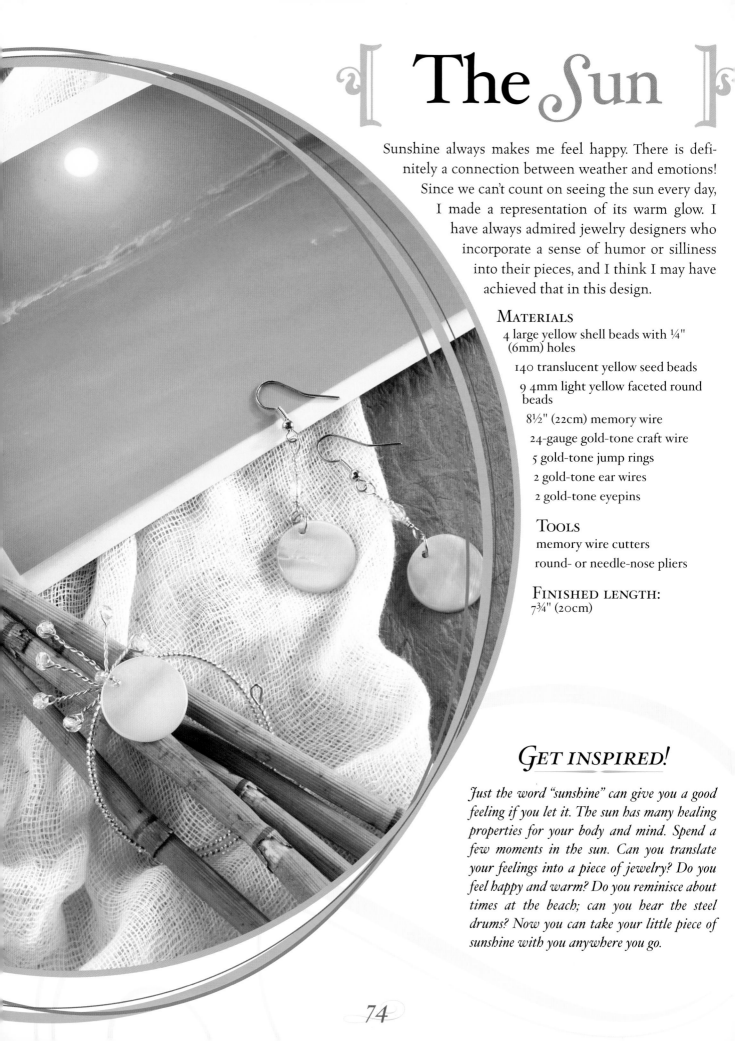

GET INSPIRED!

Just the word "sunshine" can give you a good feeling if you let it. The sun has many healing properties for your body and mind. Spend a few moments in the sun. Can you translate your feelings into a piece of jewelry? Do you feel happy and warm? Do you reminisce about times at the beach; can you hear the steel drums? Now you can take your little piece of sunshine with you anywhere you go.

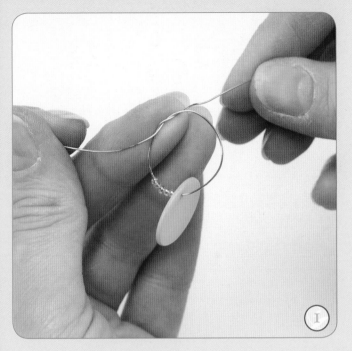

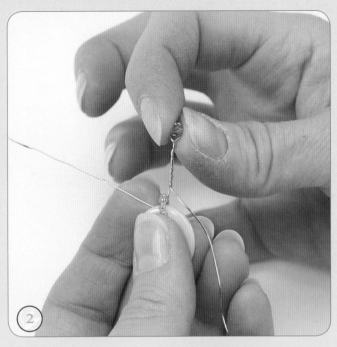

1. Begin pendant

Using wire cutters, cut a 20" (51cm) piece of 24-gauge craft wire. Thread the wire through the hole in the yellow shell bead. Add five seed beads to one end of the wire (this is now considered the front of the yellow shell bead). Tie an overhand knot (see Tying an Overhand Knot on page 12) to secure the beads in place. Bring both ends of wire to the back of the shell bead.

2. Make rays

Make the sun's rays by adding a 4mm light yellow faceted bead to one piece of wire, ¾" (2cm) above the shell bead. Fold the wire over and gently twist the two sides together.

3. Continue making rays

Repeat Step 2 to create two more sun rays.

4. Finish rays

Using the other length of wire, add three additional rays by following Steps 2 and 3. Bring the remaining wires together in the back and twist.

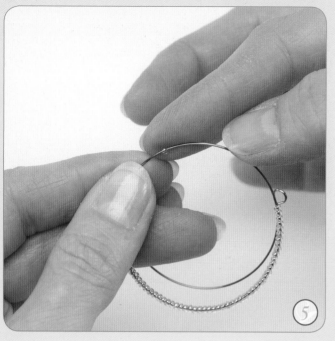

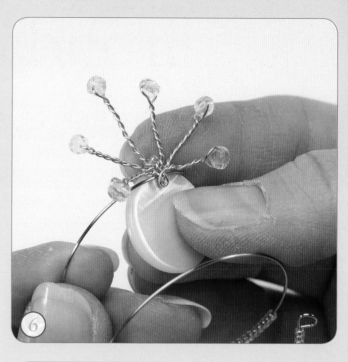

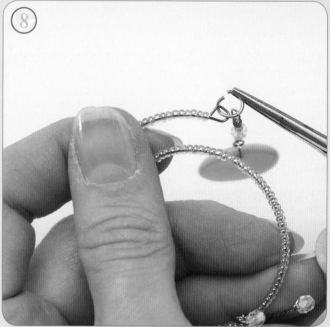

5. BEGIN BRACELET

Trim any excess wire from the sun pendant.

Using the memory wire cutters, cut an 8½" (22cm) piece of wire. Make a loop at one end (see Making a Loop on page 13). String on approximately seventy yellow seed beads, or enough to reach the middle of the memory wire.

6. ADD PENDANT

Slide the sun pendant onto the memory wire. Add approximately seventy yellow seed beads to the remaining memory wire and make a loop to finish.

7. ASSEMBLE EARRINGS AND BRACELET DANGLE

These three pieces are made in the same manner, but two are attached to ear wires and one is attached to a split ring.

Attach a gold jump ring to a shell bead. Cut a piece of craft wire approximately 2" (5cm). Loop the craft wire (see Making a Wire-Wrapped Loop on page 14) around the jump ring. To the wire, add a seed bead, 4mm yellow bead and seed bead. Make another wrapped loop. Add a jump ring. Repeat for other earring.

Repeat this pattern for the dangle, but replace the ear wire with a split ring.

8. ATTACH DANGLE

Attach the dangle to one of the bracelet loops.

Adirondack Chair

The red Adirondack chair with the palm tree resting by its side represents a trip to Florida I took in between two Ohio blizzards. We left the morning after 18 inches (46cm) of snow had fallen and returned as a new 10-inch (25cm) snowstorm began. Needless to say, those days in between were heavenly. The hotel on the beach had a group of red Adirondack chairs placed beneath a grove of palm trees. It was a great spot for relaxing.

MATERIALS
Bracelet
6 15mm green dagger beads
47 small green dagger beads
4 4mm chrysolite bicones
4 6mm peridot bicones
5 1" (3cm) wooden beads
.12 beading wire
28-gauge silver-tone craft wire
1 lobster claw clasp
2 crimp tubes
1 silver split ring

Dangle
3 15mm green dagger beads
3 small green dagger beads
2 4mm chrysolite bicones
1 silver eyepin
1 silver split ring

TOOLS
red acrylic outdoor craft paint
paintbrush
wooden skewers
crimping tool
wire cutters

FINISHED LENGTH: 7¼" (18cm)

GET INSPIRED!

If you are familiar with the mind-over-matter technique of "going to your happy place," then you are on your way to creating a unique piece of jewelry you can wear anytime you need a bit of help getting there! Whether it's a beach, an amusement park, your wedding day, sailing in a boat or visiting a cozy mountain lodge, it is possible to design a piece of jewelry to represent that.

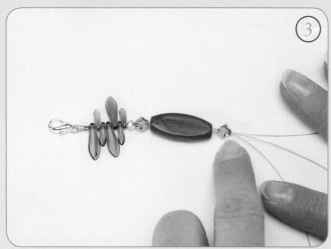

1. PAINT WOODEN BEADS

Place the wooden beads on the ends of wooden skewers, one bead for each skewer. Paint all the wooden beads using acrylic outdoor paint. Allow them to dry completely.

TIP

Place the skewers bead-end up in a tall glass to allow the beads to dry without getting paint everywhere.

2. ATTACH BEADS

Cut a 2' (61cm) piece of 28-gauge craft wire. Add a painted bead, leaving a 1" (3cm) tail.

Hold three painted beads together and weave the wire in and out through all three beads twice to link them together. Twist the two wire ends together. Trim any excess wire and press the cut ends into one of the painted beads.

3. BEGIN STRINGING

Cut three 9" (23cm) strands of beading wire. Thread the wires onto a lobster claw clasp and secure the clasp and wires with a crimp tube (see Using Crimp Beads or Tubes on page 12).

Over all three strands, string one large dagger bead, two small dagger beads, two large dagger beads, two small dagger beads, one 4mm bicone, one 6mm bicone, one wooden bead and one 6mm bicone.

4. STRING ON MORE DAGGER BEADS

Separate the three beading wires. On each of the three wires, string six small dagger beads.

5. ADD LARGE WOODEN BEAD STACK

Thread on the stack of three beads you created in Step 2, with each wire going through the corresponding holes of the stack.

Repeat the pattern from Steps 3 and 4 in reverse to complete the bracelet, this time adding a silver split ring to the other end.

6. CREATE DANGLE

Add one large dagger bead to the loop of a silver eyepin and close.

Add the following beads to the eyepin: one 4mm bicone, two small dagger beads, two large dagger beads, 1 small dagger bead and one 4mm bicone.

Turn the remaining wire to form a loop around a silver split ring and trim (see Making a Loop on page 13).

7. ADD DANGLE

Add the dangle by connecting the split rings at the end of the dangle and bracelet (see Connecting Split Rings on page 15).

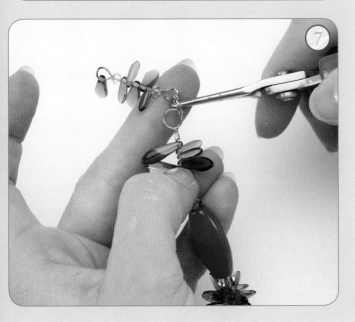

Summer Salad

One of the great aspects of summer is the abundance of fresh veggies it produces! My favorite summer salad is very basic. It wasn't until I thought about what I love and am grateful for that I considered making this into a piece of jewelry. I didn't recognize how beautifully the colors and shapes play off each other in my bowl until I started working on this. Maybe that's why I love making salads so much: They are like little pieces of artwork, beautifully balanced and arranged in a bowl.

MATERIALS

6 leaf-shaped beads (lettuce)

5 green flat, round beads (cucumbers)

7-8 red-orange, diamond-shaped beads (tomatoes)

15-20 light green glass chips (onions)

26-gauge silver-tone craft wire

6½" (17cm) stainless steel fork

TOOLS

vice grip

towel

wire cutters

FINISHED LENGTH:
7" (18cm)

GET INSPIRED!

Do you have a favorite food or beverage? It might be something you enjoy every day or look forward to ordering at a certain restaurant. Some things that come to mind are morning coffee, an apple a day or pizza on Friday night. Wouldn't it be fun to work this into a piece of jewelry? Think about the colors, shapes and textures when choosing beads or charms.

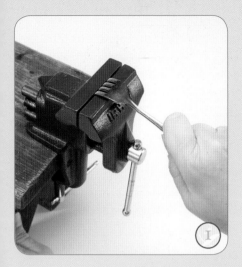

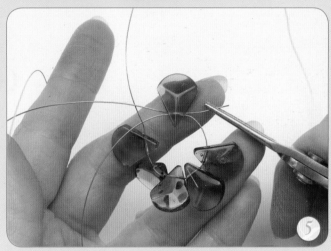

1. BEND FORK

Using your hands, straighten the neck of a fork.

Attach a vice grip to a sturdy work surface. Place the tines of the fork in the vice so the lower ¾ of the tines are in the grip. Tighten the vice. Pull the fork toward you, bending the tines where the vice closes over them. Bend the tines approximately 90°.

2. BEND TINES INTO V-SHAPE

Take the fork out of the vice. Place a towel over a flat, sturdy work surface. Place the tines of the fork onto the towel as shown above. Using your own strength, press the fork down to bend the tines into a V-shape.

TIP

Be cautious not to bend so hard that the metal begins to split.

3. CLOSE TINES

Place the V-shaped portion of the fork into the vice. Slowly tighten the vice to bend the tines until they are flat. Slightly bend the neck of the fork.

4. CREATE CUFF

To create the cuff, place the fork into the vice starting with the portion of the handle that is closest to the tines. Gently pull on the fork to curve it. Reposition the fork at ½" (1cm) intervals until it is shaped to fit your wrist.

5. STRING ON LETTUCE BEADS

Using wire cutters, cut 3' (1m) of 26-gauge craft wire.

Add six lettuce beads to the middle of the wire. Form a circle by threading one end of wire through the last bead in the opposite direction.

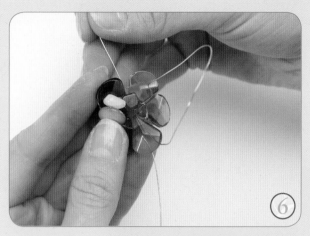

6. Sew remaining beads

Bring one end of the wire up through the middle of the circle of lettuce beads. Add a cucumber bead. Position the bead as desired. Push the wire down through the center of the lettuce bead circle and back up, wrapping the wire around the lettuce bead wire.

Add cucumber, onion and tomato beads in the manner described above.

7. Secure beads

When you have achieved the desired look, bring both wire ends to the underside of the piece. Twist the wire together to secure the beads.

8. Add beads to fork

Place the beads on top of the bent fork. Weave one strand of the wire through the tines in one direction.

9. Secure salad

Use the other strand of wire to weave in and out of the fork tines in the opposite direction. When the "salad" is secured to the fork tines, join the wires and twist them together. Weave the wires back through the fork and up through the beads.

Using the wire cutters, trim any excess wire. Give the salad at least one half twist to tighten.

Alternate Metal Cuff

If you can't find the right fork at a flea market or in your silverware drawer, you can always use a silver-plated bracelet that comes with holes in a circular pattern for sewing on beads.

Just sew the salad piece on the cuff by taking the wire through the holes until four sides are secured.

Twist the two ends together, weave them back up through the salad and trim.

Caribbean Cruise

I came across this photo taken from a small transport boat that took us from our anchored cruise ship to our port of call in Cozumel, Mexico, and was amazed by the colors. The blues in this photo and the joy of the experience made me want to commemorate the trip in a piece of jewelry.

I searched high and low for the right beads to capture this moment. I had never twisted beads together on wire in this manner, but it seemed like the only way to create the feeling of water and waves with the sun shining on them. The cruise ship charm was the perfect find to complete this memory.

MATERIALS

5g silver-lined seed beads

24 6mm dark aqua faceted beads

40 4mm light aqua faceted beads

15 aqua-lined octagonal glass beads

1 silver cruise ship charm

24-gauge silver-tone craft wire

1 silver-tone lobster claw clasp

2 silver-tone split rings

1 silver-tone eyepin

TOOLS

wire cutters

round-nose pliers

FINISHED LENGTH:

7½" (19cm)

GET INSPIRED!

"What's your favorite color?" You have probably been asked this question many times and immediately know the answer. Do you know why you are drawn to a color or a color combination? The memories attached to favorite colors are the perfect inspiration for a piece of jewelry.

1. Prepare wires

Cut three 14" (36cm) pieces of 24-gauge craft wire. Pull all three wires through the end of the lobster claw clasp. Wrap the end around the three wires tightly at least twice. Trim any excess wire.

2. Thread on beads

String beads as follows:

Strand 1: alternate 4mm beads and 6mm beads using twenty-three of each bead.

Strand 2: alternate 4mm beads and octagonal beads using fifteen 4mm beads and fourteen octagonal beads.

Strand 3: string silver-lined seed beads to the same length as the other strands.

At the end of each strand, lightly twist the ends of the wires to temporarily secure the beads.

3. Twist together strands 1 and 2

Starting at the clasp, twist strands 1 and 2 together.

4. Wrap strand 3 around twist

Go back to the clasp and twist strand 3 over strands 1 and 2. Add seed beads to lengthen as needed to reach the end.

5. ADD SPLIT RING

Remove the temporary twists from the ends of the wires. Hold the three wires together and twist them tightly two to three times.

Take the twisted strands through a split ring and wire-wrap them as you did in Step 1. Trim any excess wire.

6. CREATE DANGLE

Open the loop of the eyepin and add the cruise ship charm.

Add the following to the eyepin: 4mm bead, 6mm bead, seed bead, octagonal bead, seed bead and 4mm bead.

7. ADD DANGLE

Make a loop at the end of the eyepin (see Making a Loop on page 13). Add a split ring to this loop.

Connect the split rings of the dangle and the bracelet (see Connecting Split Rings on page 15).

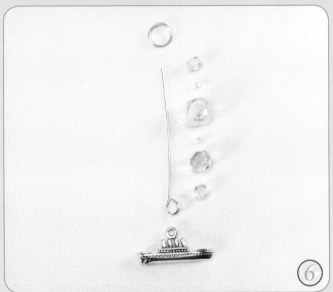

Hug a Dolphin

My dolphin encounter in the Bahamas is one of my most cherished memories. I didn't think I was adventurous enough to go through with it, but with enough encouragement, I agreed. It was a gorgeous day for the boat ride to Blue Lagoon Island where these dolphins live—they are not in captivity, but choose to participate for the fun and the food! It was an amazing experience to meet these lovable creatures, and now I have more than just pictures to help me remember it. Finding this "dolphin" bead was almost as exciting as the original encounter.

MATERIALS
Necklace
- 5 gray glass beads (dolphins)
- 110 4mm gray top-drilled pearls
- 48 3mm clear faceted AB beads
- .12 Soft Flex beading wire
- 1" (3cm) silver-tone chain
- 2 silver-tone split rings
- 1 silver-tone lobster claw clasp
- 4 crimp tubes

Dangle
- 2 4mm gray top-drilled pearls
- 1 3mm clear faceted AB bead
- 1 silver-tone headpin

TOOLS
- crimping tool
- needle-nose pliers
- wire cutters

FINISHED LENGTH:
17½" (45cm)

GET INSPIRED!

Is there a once-in-a-lifetime experience you are dreaming about or in the process of planning? A piece of jewelry will help maintain your excitement until that day arrives. If it's only a dream, creating this piece will help you stay focused on it to help it come true. Take some notes as you create this experience in your mind so you are prepared when you begin hunting for beads.

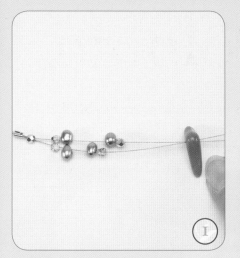

1. Prepare short beaded strand

Cut 13" (33cm) of beading wire. Fold the wire in half and slide a crimp tube over both wires. Push the crimp tube up to the end of the doubled wire until it forms a small loop. Use the crimping tool to secure the crimp tube. Place a faceted bead, two pearls and a faceted bead on each of the two strands separately. String a dolphin bead over both strands.

2. Finish short strand

Place a faceted bead, a pearl and a faceted bead on each of the two strands and add a dolphin bead over both strands. Repeat the pattern three times. After the fifth dolphin bead, place a faceted bead, two pearls and a faceted bead on each of the two strands separately. String a faceted bead and a crimp tube over both strands.

Make a loop in the beading wire and use needle-nose pliers to hold the loop while tucking the two strands back through the crimp tube. Use the crimping tool to secure the crimp tube. Trim the wires at the crimp tube.

3. Begin long necklace strand

Cut a 17" (43cm) piece of beading wire for the necklace. Slide a crimp tube over one end of the wire, add the lobster claw clasp and run the wire back through the crimp tube. Use the crimping tool to flatten the crimp tube.

String a faceted bead and five pearls onto the wire.

4. String on short strand

Repeat the pattern from Step 3 six times. Add the short beaded strand from Step 1 by running the necklace wire through one of the end loops.

5. Fill in space with beads

Add a faceted bead and five pearls. Repeat this pattern four times. Add a faceted bead and take the necklace wire through the other end of the short beaded strand.

6. FINISH NECKLACE

Add a faceted bead and five pearls. Repeat this pattern six times and add a final faceted bead. String on the final crimp tube and split ring. Run the wire back through the crimp tube and faceted bead. Use the crimping tool to flatten the crimp tube. Trim any excess wire. Add a 1" (3cm) piece of silver chain to the split ring. Add the final split ring to the end of the chain.

7. ADD DANGLE

Add a faceted bead, two pearls and a faceted bead to a headpin. Make a loop and trim any excess wire.

Connect the dangle to the split ring at the end of the silver chain (see Connecting Split Rings on page 15).

Variation: Hug a Dolphin Ring

These dolphin beads were so adorable, I wanted to use one of them in a corresponding piece of jewelry. The ring allows one dolphin to be showcased as if it is jumping out of the water. The sparkly faceted beads represent the water bubbles the dolphin creates as it crashes back into the water.

MATERIALS
1 gray glass bead (dolphin)
12–14 3mm clear faceted AB beads
2 4mm gray top-drilled pearls
1 silver-tone ring with 3 loops
14" (36cm) 28-gauge silver-tone craft wire

1. ATTACH WIRE
Run one end of the craft wire through the end loop of the ring form and wrap twice to secure.

2. ADD BEADS
Add beads to the wire randomly and wrap around the ring to form a bauble. At the midpoint, add a dolphin bead so it sits on top of the bauble.

3. SECURE BEADS AND WIRE
Continue adding random beads and wrapping the wire around the ring form. Wrap the wire several times through the last loop and trim any excess wire.

Furry Family Members

As a dog lover and "parent" to two dogs, I thought it would be fun to create a representation of them in a piece of jewelry. For this project, the beads had to be white, and I wanted to add a little sparkle. The challenge was to create a design that would not be too juvenile. I was hoping to come up with something pretty that would get a double take with a smile when people realize it's a dog. I can't help but smile when I catch a glimpse of the finished bracelet on my wrist. The nice thing is there's no barking or begging involved!

MATERIALS

31 6mm white opal faceted
1 6mm white opal drop crystal
12 6mm white opal AB bicones
1 6mm comet argent bicone
1 4mm black diamond bicone
8 4mm clear AB bicones
54 crystal seed beads
.12 silver satin fine beading wire
2 silver-tone crimp tubes
1 silver-tone ball clasp
4 silver-tone headpins

TOOLS

wire cutters

FINISHED LENGTH:

6½" (17cm)

GET INSPIRED!

Have you ever noticed that you feel more whimsical on some days than others? One day, you might be in a conservative mood and wear a buttoned-down blouse and simple jewelry. On other days, you throw caution to the wind and break out the most silly, colorful and dangly piece of jewelry you have! The next time you are feeling whimsical, try to figure out what put you in that mood. Then break out the beads and try to re-create that in a piece of jewelry.

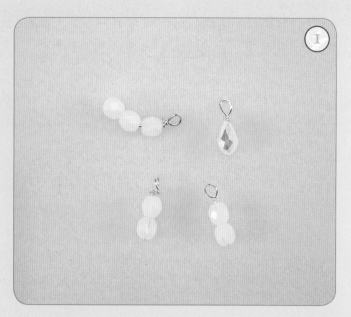

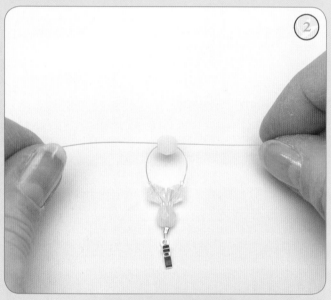

1. MAKE PUPPY PIECES

Make the pieces that will become the ear, legs and tail of the dog as follows:

Ear: place the white opal drop crystal on a silver headpin and make a wire-wrapped loop (see Making a Wire-Wrapped Loop on page 14).

Tail: place three white opal faceted beads on a silver headpin and make a wire-wrapped loop.

Legs (make two): place two white opal faceted beads on a silver headpin and make a wire-wrapped loop.

2. BEGIN BEADED PATTERN

Cut one 18" (46cm) piece of beading wire. Fold it in half and add a crimp tube and clasp onto one end. Use a crimping tool to secure the crimp tube. Add a white opal faceted bead over both wires. Separate the two wires and add a seed bead, 6mm white opal bicone and a seed bead to each of the strands. Add a white opal faceted bead to the left wire and take the right wire through the same white opal faceted bead from right to left.

3. ADD PUPPY TAIL

Repeat Step 2 twice. Add a seed bead, 4mm clear AB bicone and a seed bead to each wire. Add a 4mm clear bicone to both wires. Pull the two wires apart gently and on each strand add a seed bead, 4mm clear bicone and a seed bead.

Add a white opal faceted bead onto the left strand and take the right strand through the same bead from right to left. On the wire sitting on the top side of your piece, add a seed bead and the tail piece from Step 1.

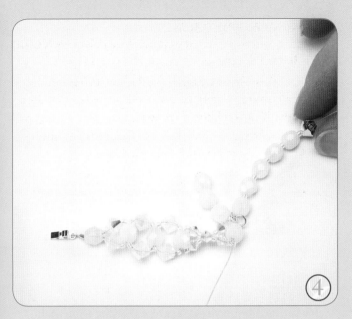

4. Continue beading

Add five more combinations of seed beads and white opal faceted beads until you have five faceted beads following the tail. Add a seed bead and a 6mm comet argent bicone.

5. Add puppy legs

On the wire sitting to the bottom side of your piece, add a seed bead and one leg piece. Complete three more combinations of seed beads and white opal faceted beads. Add the other leg.

6. Complete body

Add a white opal faceted bead and a seed bead after the leg piece. Bring the bottom wire through the 6mm comet argent bicone that is connected to the top of the piece (from right to left).

7. Join body and begin head

Pull the wires to join the upper and lower portions of the body. The bottom wire is now the top wire.

On the top wire add a seed bead, white opal faceted bead, seed bead, ear piece, white opal faceted bead, seed bead, white opal faceted bead, seed bead and a 4mm black diamond bicone.

8. Finish puppy head

On the bottom wire add a seed bead, white opal faceted bead, seed bead, white opal faceted bead, seed bead, white opal faceted bead and a seed bead. Take the bottom wire through the black diamond bicone from right to left.

9. Secure head with beads

Bring the two wires together and add a 4mm clear bicone over both wires. Separate the wires. On each wire add a seed bead, 4mm clear bicone and a seed bead.

10. Begin pattern

Turn the piece 90° counterclockwise. The top wire becomes the left wire; the bottom wire becomes the right wire. Add an opal faceted bead on the left wire and bring the right wire through the same opal faceted bead from right to left.

11. Finish bead pattern

On each strand add a seed bead, 6mm opal bicone and a seed bead. Add an opal faceted bead to the left wire and bring the right wire through the same round opal from right to left.

Repeat once.

Bring the two wires together and add an opal faceted bead over both of them. Add a crimp tube and clasp. Thread the wires back down through the last opal faceted bead.

12. Secure bracelet

Pull the wires to tighten the beadwork and use the crimping tool to flatten the crimp tube (see Using Crimp Beads or Tubes on page 12).

Using wire cutters, trim any excess wire.

[Candy Dish]

Candy serves many purposes. It is fun to eat and to look at. It takes you back to childhood and sets a jovial tone. This bracelet uses a variety of beads from my endless supply of odds and ends. I went through all of my stashes of beads and pulled out the colors and shapes that reminded me of my favorite candy. Anyone with a bead obsession will understand the joy of picking through your bead collections for specific colors and shapes.

MATERIALS
33 candy-like beads
24-gauge silver-tone craft wire
1 3-strand silver-tone bar clasp

TOOLS
wire cutters
round-nose pliers
flat-nose pliers

FINISHED LENGTH:
7½" (19cm)

GET INSPIRED!

Candy comes in so many varieties these days—sweet, sour, hard, chewy and powdery. In addition to the ever-growing selection of new candies, there are entire stores that cater to retro or novelty candy. Anything that fizzes or pops is a favorite of mine! The next time you peruse the candy store or aisle, look for a bit of jewelry inspiration—I guarantee you won't have to look far.

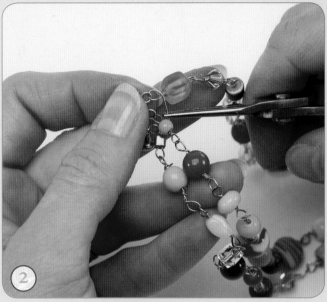

1. BEGIN ADDING RANDOM BEADS

Cut thirty-three 2½" (6cm) pieces of wire. Run a piece of wire through one of the holes on the bar clasp. Make a wire-wrapped loop (see Making a Wire-Wrapped Loop on page 14).

Add a bead to the wire and make a wire-wrapped loop on the other end. Run the end of the next piece of wire through the previously wrapped loop and make a wire-wrapped loop to link them together.

2. COMPLETE BRACELET

Repeat Step 1 until you have eleven wire-wrapped beads. Finish by making a wire-wrapped loop to connect the strands to the other end of the clasp after the eleventh bead. Repeat for the other two strands.

*T*IP

To get the desired result, determine the layout before linking the beads together.

❦[*V*ariation: Candy Dish Earrings]❦

This candy bracelet needs some colorful, fun earrings to go with it! I think the round red beads are cheerful and representative of candy. They complement the bracelet nicely.

MATERIALS

2 8mm round red beads
2 4mm peridot bicones
2 6/0 yellow seed beads
2 silver ear wires
6 headpins

1. ADD BEADS TO HEADPINS

On two headpins, slide on one peridot bicone. Trim wire approximately ⅜" (1cm) above bead and make loop.

2. CREATE BEAD SECTIONS

Eyepins can be alternately used for each of these sections, but headpins can be used by trimming off the head. On two of the headpins, make a loop on the end of the headpin, trim off the head and slide on a red bead. Trim the wire down to approximately ⅜" (1cm) above the bead and make a loop.

Repeat this step for two additional headpins using one yellow 6/0 E bead on each.

3. ASSEMBLE EARRINGS

Beginning with one of the peridot headpins, gently open the loop, connect one of the red bead section loops and close the loop.

Gently open the top loop on the red bead section, slide on a yellow bead section loop and close the loop.

Open the top loop on the yellow bead section, slide on the ear wire loop and close the loop.

Box of Chocolates

I was about to give in to a chocolate craving when I decided it would be more calorie-conscious to wear the chocolates rather than eat them. There is something so festive and special about a box of chocolates. When I discovered these multicolored discs with swirls on them, I decided they would work well as the chocolates. Then, I just needed a "box" to put them in. Creating structural elements can be challenging, but it's rewarding when you finally figure it out! Have your bead catalogs handy, or take a quick trip to the craft store to get your imagination going.

MATERIALS
82 4mm jet black Swarovski crystals

8 3-hole jet black glass spacers

7 glass 8mm × 3mm coin beads with swirls

Soft Flex beading wire

1 3-hole silver-tone bar clasp

6 silver-tone crimp tubes

TOOLS
flat-nose pliers

wire cutters

FINISHED LENGTH:
7" (18cm)

GET INSPIRED!

I don't think I have ever met someone who didn't like chocolate in some form—cake, cookies, candy or a chocolatey drink. The next time you are eating chocolate with someone, ask them to describe their experience. Did you ever think there were so many thoughts and emotions tangled up in eating chocolate? Using that inspiration, put together something that expresses the experience.

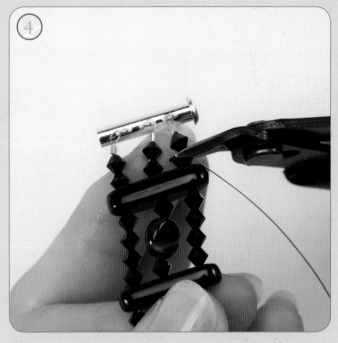

1. BEGIN BRACELET

Cut three 9" (23cm) pieces of wire. Add crimp tubes to each wire. Thread each of the three wires through the corresponding hole of the bar clasp and back through the crimp tubes. Crimp the tubes to secure the wires (see Using Crimp Beads or Tubes on page 12).

On each wire, string two crystals. Add a glass spacer to all three wires.

2. BEGIN PATTERN

String the following pattern:

On each outside strand, string four crystals.

On the middle wire, string a crystal, coin bead and a crystal. Over all three wires, string a glass spacer.

3. FINISH BEADING

Repeat the pattern in Step 2 until you have used a total of eight glass spacers. Add two crystals to each wire.

4. SECURE BRACELET

Add crimp tubes to each wire. Thread each of the three wires through the corresponding hole of the bar clasp, then back through the crimp tube and the last bead. Crimp the crimp tubes to secure the wires. Using wire cutters, trim the excess wire.

Mosaic Tile

Blue has always been my favorite color. As a child, I wanted to paint my ceiling sky blue with puffy white clouds. I'm still drawn to the color blue and especially objects with various shades of blue and white. The cheerfulness of these colors translates well on the slick, shiny surface of tile.

After I learned how to use the peyote stitch with glass cubes, this project was an absolute must! You can make this bracelet as wide as you like and with as many variations of color as you can find. Once you get the hang of this stitch, you might not be able to stop.

MATERIALS
61 3mm black AB cubes
21 3mm light blue cubes
25 3mm teal-lined cubes
40 3mm sky-blue-lined cubes
20 3mm clear AB cubes
16 3mm silver-lined cubes
16 3mm pewter-lined cubes
15 clear seed beads
1 stop bead
beading thread
1 button (for closure)

TOOLS
beading needle
cutting tool
Super Glue

FINISHED LENGTH:
7" (18cm)

GET INSPIRED!

Are you drawn to certain patterns or colors? Look around while shopping, walking down the street or even around your own kitchen. What colors inspire you or give you a boost? I like to use my cell phone for taking photos of things I come across in daily life. Fruits and vegetables displayed neatly in the grocery store inspire wonderful color combinations!

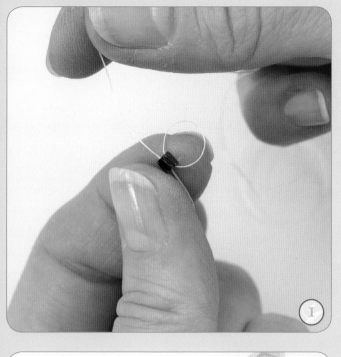

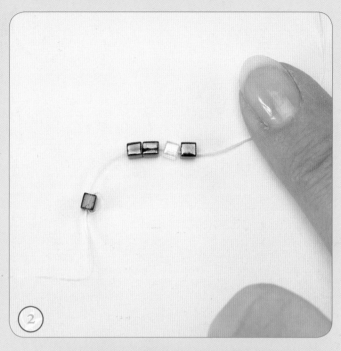

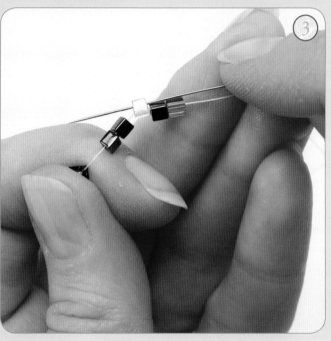

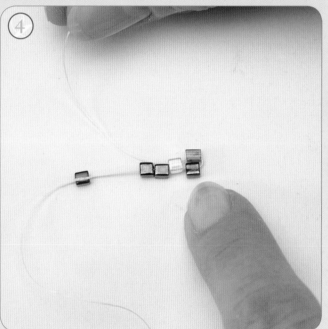

1. ADD STOP BEAD

Cut 3' (1m) of beading thread. Add the needle and the stop bead, leaving an 8" (20cm) tail. Pull the thread to secure the stop bead.

2. ADD FOUNDATION ROW

String on a random mix of four cubes.

3. BEGIN SECOND ROW

Add one cube. Maneuver it so it sits on top of the fourth bead of the foundation row.

4. SECURE BEAD

Working from right to left, hold the bead in place and take the needle through the second bead of the foundation row.

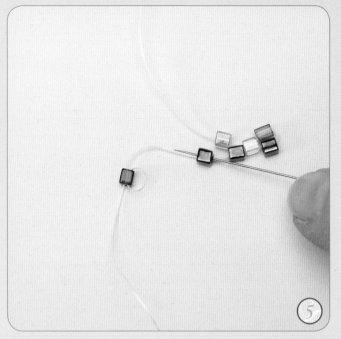

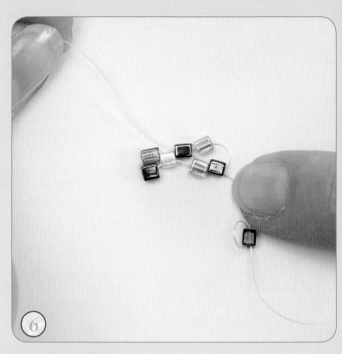

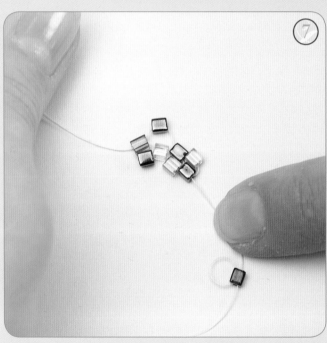

5. COMPLETE ROW 2

Add a bead so it sits on top of the third bead in the foundation row and pass the needle through the first bead of the foundation row.

6. BEGIN ROW 3

Flip the beads so the working thread is on the right. String on a bead and let it sit on the first bead of the foundation row. Thread the needle through the first bead of row 2.

7. CONTINUE PATTERN

Continue adding beads in this manner to the desired length.

8. SECURE BEADWORK

After the final bead is added, the thread will be coming out the right side. (If needed, flip the beadwork so the thread comes out the right side). Take the needle through the far right bead on the second row down and bring it back up between the third and fourth bead in that row.

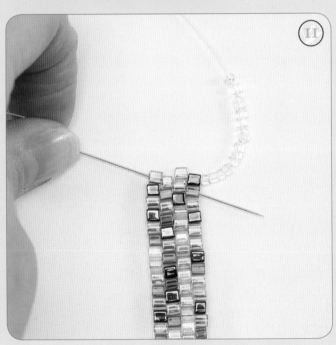

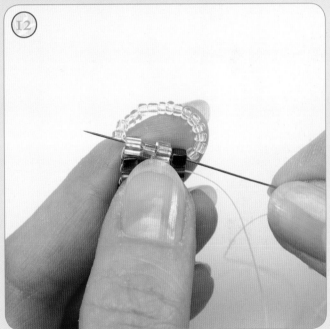

9. STRING ON BUTTON
Thread on a cube, the button and another cube.

10. SECURE BUTTON
Take the needle through the third bead down on the left side. Continue weaving in and out of beads, bringing the needle and thread back through the cube/button/cube formation to secure the button. Knot the thread in various places to secure the button. Add a dot of Super Glue if desired. When the button is secure, trim the thread.

11. BEGIN LOOP
Remove the stop bead from the other end of the bracelet. Add the needle to the thread. String on fifteen seed beads. Take the needle diagonally to the right, as shown, so the needle comes back out through the first bead in row 2.

12. SECURE LOOP
Take the needle through the entire first row to secure the loop.

13. MEASURE BUTTON

Check the loop size by taking it over the button. If it fits securely, pull the thread through several rows of cubes and go back through the seed beads to anchor the loop.

14. ANCHOR LOOP

Anchor the loop by going through all the seed beads.

15. REINFORCE LOOP

Take the needle through the first row of cube beads one last time to secure.

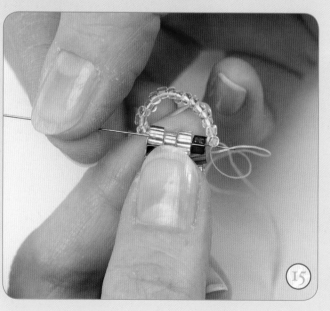

16. SECURE THREAD

Take the needle through the looped thread on the outside of the first row of beads to form a couple of overhand knots to secure the thread (see Tying an Overhand Knot on page 12).

17. HIDE THREAD

After knotting, take the needle through the entire first row.

18. TRIM THREAD

Pull the thread tight and trim the excess.

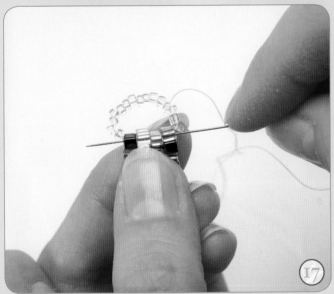

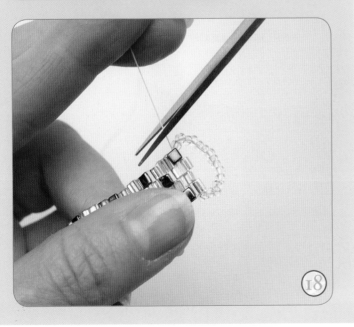

Chapter 4: Funky Finds

I'm guessing I'm not the only one who has a quirky side. I like things that are fun, unique and a bit off-kilter. Several projects in this chapter were inspired by materials found in the sewing-related aisles of the craft store. Taking a stroll down the ribbon, button and iron-on aisles is a great way to change your perspective and challenge your creativity with regard to making jewelry.

The important thing when strolling the aisles is to be open to anything and everything. I got stuck in the ribbon and button aisles, checking out all of the little works of art. Consequently, ribbons and buttons are the focal points in several projects in this chapter, including *Ribbon and Chain* (see page 106) and *Button Necklace* (see page 112). A walk down the scrapbook aisle led to the funky *Gnome Chain Necklace* (see page 115). Other projects were inspired by kitschy pieces I have collected: *50s Holiday Wreath* (see page 120) and *Tinsel Tree* (see page 118).

I would love to see what you come up with and share your "funky finds" crafty jewelry on my blog at www.abeadaday.blogspot.com. Stop by and leave a note or send me an e-mail.

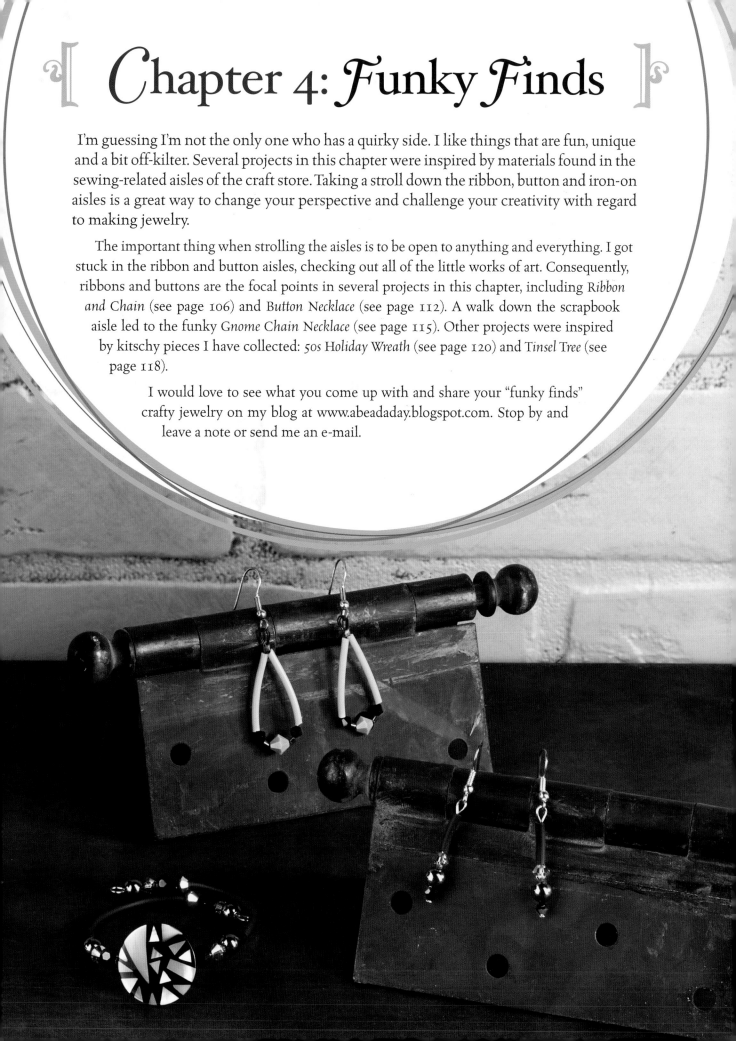

Ribbon and Chain

Craft stores offer endless inspiration if you keep your mind open. I came across some great ribbon varieties, but I wasn't sure how to incorporate them into jewelry pieces. After experimenting and discovering the ribbon clasp, it all came together.

You can make a bracelet for all your friends— they're quick to complete and require very basic jewelry-making skills. The blue and silver ribbon is the first one I selected, and I loved the resulting bracelet so much that I slept in it! It reminded me of a piece of artwork in a bright silver frame.

MATERIALS
ribbon

4½" (11cm) silver chain

1 silver-tone magnetic clasp

1 pair ¾" (2cm) silver ribbon crimps

4 silver jump rings

iron-on patch material, cut to size of ribbon

TOOLS
wire cutters

needle-nose pliers

scissors

iron

ironing board

FINISHED LENGTH:
7" (18cm)

GET INSPIRED!

If you already have a collection of interesting ribbon or fabric, you could easily spend a Saturday designing a unique piece of jewelry. Consider using snap or button closures for wide ribbon cuffs, or even using fabric pieces to fashion a mini patchwork design. Using extra denim as a bracelet base, the sky is the limit as to how much embellishment you can add.

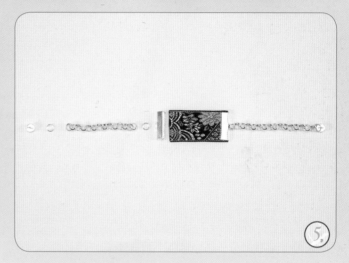

1. CUT MATERIALS
Cut a 1¾" × 1" (4cm × 3cm) piece of ribbon. Cut iron-on patch material to the same size as the ribbon.

2. ADHERE RIBBON AND PATCH
Following the manufacturer's instructions, place the ribbon face down on the ironing board, add the patch adhesive-side down and press gently. Allow it to cool.

3. CUT CHAIN
Using wire cutters, cut two 2¼" (6cm) pieces of silver chain, cutting at the soldered part of the link.

4. ATTACH CRIMP
Position one of the ribbon crimps on the end of the ribbon piece and flatten gently with pliers.

5. ASSEMBLE BRACELET
Repeat Step 4 on the other end. Add a jump ring and length of chain (see Opening and Closing Jump Rings on page 15) to each of the ribbon crimps. Add a jump ring and magnetic clasp to the other ends of the chain.

TIP

If the ribbon clasp you choose has visible "teeth" on only one side, these should be positioned to the back of the bracelet for a more finished look on the front.

Focal Button

It can be frustrating to explore the many types of crafts and hobbies, only to discover the amount of time it would take to learn and eventually master them. As a result, when I see pretty or sparkly things, I wonder how I could use them to make jewelry instead. This button is so gorgeous it (almost) made me want to take up sewing!

This button seemed an easy match for a one-strand memory wire bracelet with rubber tubing. This simple project can be done in less time than it takes to peruse a craft store!

MATERIALS
1 focal button with shank in black, gray and silver tones

4 6mm faceted black glass beads

4 6mm hematite round beads

6 5mm black diamond Swarovski crystals

4 4mm jet black AB Swarovski crystals

10" (25cm) memory wire

5¾" (15cm) black rubber tubing

TOOLS
round- or needle-nose pliers

heavy wire cutters or memory wire cutters

FINISHED LENGTH: 7" (18cm)

GET INSPIRED!

This is the perfect opportunity for using memory wire. Take your time finding a button that captures your spirit or makes you smile. It might be a 2" (5cm) wide daisy or a demure, faceted gem. Select a coordinating color of rubber tubing or find the perfect complement of fire polished rounds to use as a band. Be careful, this project could be addictive!

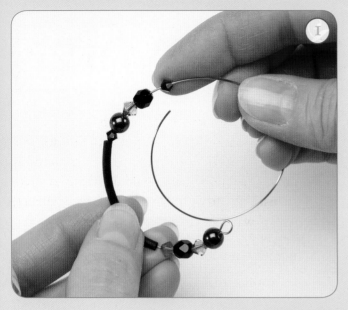

1. ADD BEADS AND TUBING

Using memory wire cutters, cut a 10" (25cm) piece of memory wire and make a loop on one end (see Making a Loop on page 13). Add the following beads: hematite bead, black diamond crystal, faceted glass bead, black diamond crystal, 2" (5cm) piece of rubber tubing, jet black crystal, hematite bead, black diamond crystal, faceted glass bead, jet black crystal, and a 2" (5cm) piece of rubber tubing.

2. PREPARE BUTTON

Slide the button onto a ¾" (2cm) piece of rubber tubing to add stability.

3. FINISH BRACELET

Slide the wire through the rubber tubing to add the button.

Add a jet black crystal, faceted glass bead, black diamond crystal, hematite bead, jet black crystal, 1" (3cm) piece of rubber tubing, black diamond crystal, faceted glass bead, black diamond crystal and a hematite bead. Cut any excess wire as needed and make a final loop.

ᵛariation: Earrings

The rubber tubing in this project provides a unique quality to the bracelet. A simple pair of earrings using the same materials will pull the two pieces together for a coordinated look.

MATERIALS

2 silver headpins
2 silver fishhook ear wires
2 ¾" pieces of rubber tubing
2 5 mm black diamond Swarovski crystals
2 6 mm hematite round beads
2 jet AB 4 mm Swarovski crystals

ASSEMBLE EARRINGS

Place beads on the headpin as follows: 4 mm jet crystal, 6 mm hematite round, 5 mm black diamond crystal and rubber tubing.

Make a loop. Add the earwire. Repeat this step for the second earring.

Rock Star Iron-On

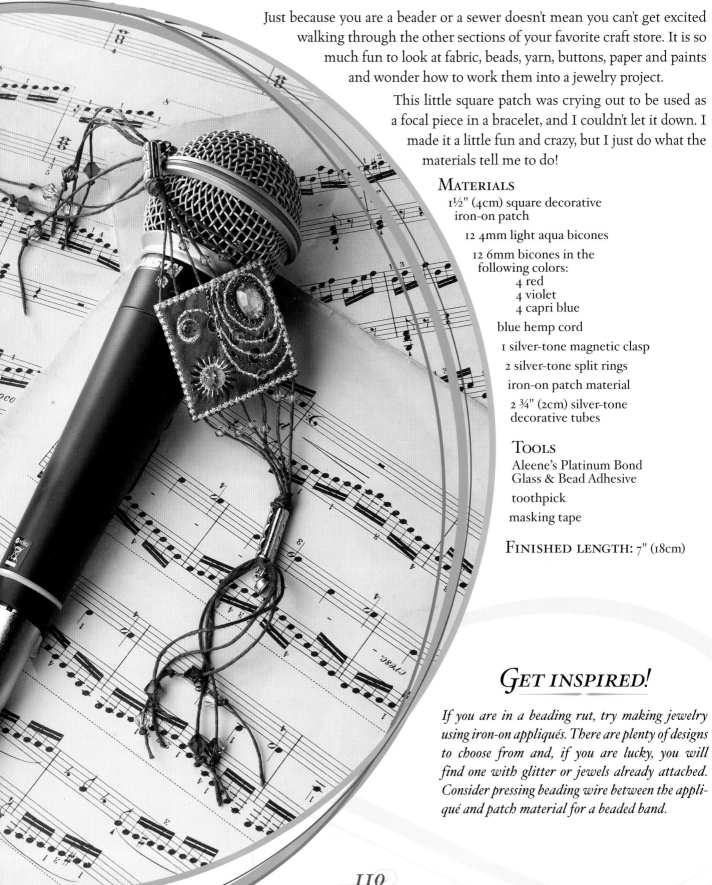

Just because you are a beader or a sewer doesn't mean you can't get excited walking through the other sections of your favorite craft store. It is so much fun to look at fabric, beads, yarn, buttons, paper and paints and wonder how to work them into a jewelry project.

This little square patch was crying out to be used as a focal piece in a bracelet, and I couldn't let it down. I made it a little fun and crazy, but I just do what the materials tell me to do!

MATERIALS
1½" (4cm) square decorative iron-on patch

12 4mm light aqua bicones

12 6mm bicones in the following colors:
    4 red
    4 violet
    4 capri blue

blue hemp cord

1 silver-tone magnetic clasp

2 silver-tone split rings

iron-on patch material

2 ¾" (2cm) silver-tone decorative tubes

TOOLS
Aleene's Platinum Bond Glass & Bead Adhesive

toothpick

masking tape

FINISHED LENGTH: 7" (18cm)

GET INSPIRED!

If you are in a beading rut, try making jewelry using iron-on appliqués. There are plenty of designs to choose from and, if you are lucky, you will find one with glitter or jewels already attached. Consider pressing beading wire between the appliqué and patch material for a beaded band.

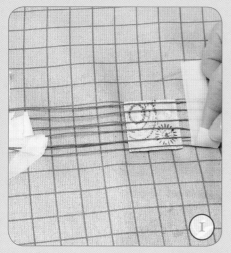

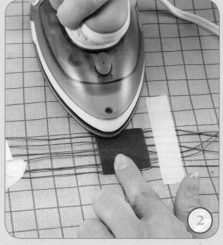

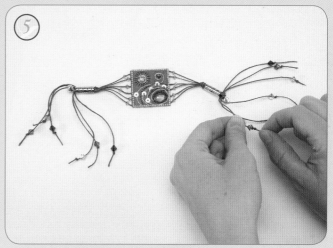

1. POSITION CORDS

Cut a piece of iron-on material to fit the back of the decorative patch. Cut six 2½' (76cm) strands of blue hemp cord. Place the iron-on patch face down on the ironing board. Position the hemp cord strands, one at a time, over the decorative patch. Secure the cord ends to the ironing board on both sides with masking tape.

2. ADHERE FABRIC AND CORDS

Position the iron-on fabric, adhesive-side down, over the hemp cords. Following the manufacturer's instructions, press the fabric gently in place. Let the fabric cool for a few minutes.

TIP

Depending on the thickness of the cord, it might be helpful to trim the ends to a point to string on the bicones.

3. SECURE CORDS

Before removing the piece from the ironing board, check to ensure the corners are adhered. Remove the piece from the ironing board and add a 4mm bicone to each strand. On one side, bring the six strands together. Ensure they are all equally straight and in place and tie an overhand knot (see Tying an Overhand Knot on page 12). Using the toothpick and Aleene's Platinum Bond Glass & Bead Adhesive, secure the knot.

4. ADD JUMP RING

Let the glue set. Repeat step 3 on the other side. Place a silver-tone tube on one side over all six strands. Slide a silver jump ring over one strand and tie all strands into a knot. Repeat on the other side.

5. FINISH BRACELET

Secure the knots on both sides with the toothpick and glue. Add a magnetic clasp to the split rings (see Opening and Closing Split Rings on page 15). Add a red, violet or blue 6mm crystal to each strand and tie an overhand knot at the end of each strand to secure the crystal. Trim any excess cording below the knot.

Button Necklace

When jewelry happens without planning, you know you are on the right track!

I was drawn to the colors and design of this large button; the size alone dictated that it should be positioned front and center on the neck. I had just ordered multiple colors of memory wire rubber tubing and the sky blue color matched this button perfectly.

I hope you will take a trip down the button aisle of your local craft store and pick something interesting that catches your eye. The challenge is then to push yourself to create something one-of-a-kind.

MATERIALS
1 large 2-hole focal button

10 6mm matte turquoise Swarovski bicone crystals

.4 mm black Tattü Magic jewelry cord

light blue rubber tubing

26 1.3mm silver crimp tubes

silver-plated lobster claw clasp

silver-plated split ring

TOOLS
wire cutters or scissors

needle-nose pliers

FINISHED LENGTH:
15" (38cm)

GET INSPIRED!

It is so much fun to shop for giant buttons! They are inexpensive and you are sure to find one that suits your style. Select one to incorporate into a cute choker or dangly necklace. Rubber tubing and colorful beading wire work great for these projects, but if you prefer a beaded necklace, give that a try, too! All of your crafty friends will want one of these, so make a few.

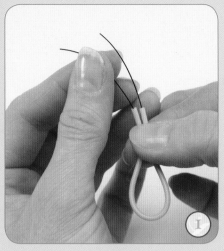

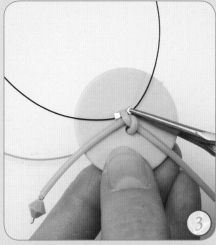

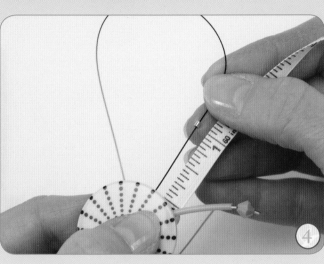

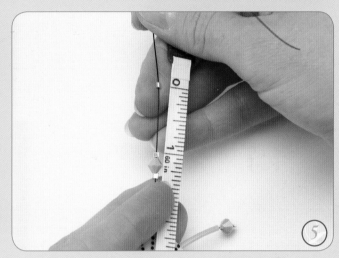

1. Prepare cording
Cut a 7" (18cm) piece of jewelry cord. Cut a 4" (10cm) piece of light blue rubber tubing. Run the cord through the rubber tubing so it is evenly spaced coming out of the ends.

2. Add button
Run each end of the tubing down through each of the button holes from the front side of the button. Once they are both behind the button, even the lengths and tie an overhand knot (see Tying an Overhand Knot on page 12). Place a crimp tube on either side of the the black wire coming out of the tubing and flatten. Add a turquoise bicone crystal and crimp tube. Flatten the crimp and trim any excess wire (see Flattening Crimp Tubes on page 12).

3. Add cording
Cut a 20" (51cm) piece of jewelry cord. Run the cord through the rubber tubing knot on the back of the button. Place a crimp tube on either side of the cord. Ensure the ends are even and flatten each crimp tube against the knot with the needle-nose pliers.

4. Measure cording
Starting on the left side, measure 1" (3cm) from the edge of the button.

5. Embellish cording
String a crimp on one strand of cording 1" (3 cm) from the edge of the button. Flatten the crimp and add a turquoise bicone. Add another crimp and flatten it to hold the bead in place. Place five bead/crimp groupings at 1" (3cm) intervals on both strands.

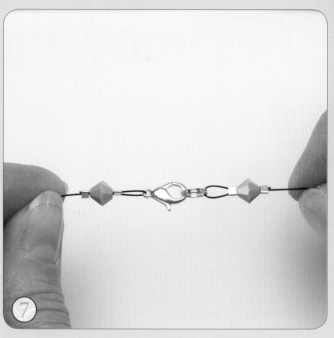

6. ADD CLASP

Place the final bead grouping on the wire, run it through the clasp and back through all three pieces. Flatten both crimps and trim any excess wire.

7. FINISH NECKLACE

Repeat for the right side. Add the other end of the clasp.

[Variation: Earrings]

Since the color combination in this necklace is unique, I thought it would be nice to have a pair of earrings to match. When creating earrings, I always try to use the same materials in the necklace or bracelet to make a jewelry "set."

MATERIALS

2 6mm matte turquoise Swarovski crystals

4 jet black bicones

2 4" (10cm) pieces black cording

4 1" (3cm) pieces sky blue rubber tubing

5 1.3mm crimp tubes

2 ear wires

1. ADD BEADS AND TUBING

String a 4mm jet black bicone, crimp tube, turquoise bicone, crimp tube, jet black bicone and a piece of rubber tubing onto a 4" (10cm) piece of cording.

Add a crimp tube over both pieces of cording.

2. FINISH EARRINGS

Arrange beads evenly and run both ends of cording through the earring wire loop and back through one of the rubber tubes.

Flatten the crimp tube. Repeat steps 1 and 2 for the other earring.

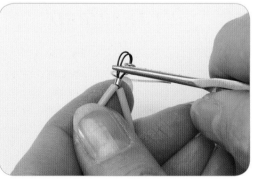

Gnome Chain Necklace

Something about these gnomes makes me chuckle, so I decided to wear the laughs! Using photos in craft projects is always fun, and the possibilities are endless.

It helps to resize and print the photos from your home computer, but you can also take photos with a project in mind and adjust your distance to your subject. If you sort through boxes or albums full of previously taken photos, you are sure to find something that fits a small frame, too. Your imagination is the only limit on this project!

MATERIALS
metal frame

DecoArt Triple Thick Gloss

15–16" (38–41cm) antique silver chain

antique silver or brushed pewter toggle

photos

decorative paper

Tupperware lid

TOOLS
2 sets of round-nose pliers

paintbrush/sponge brush

pencil

FINISHED LENGTH:
16" (41cm)

GET INSPIRED!

Incorporating photos into jewelry can make your pieces unique and meaningful. Imagine using photos of kids, pets, special events, blue sky or flowers. Once you select a photo, determining the best way to "frame" it can take a little creativity. Can you decoupage it onto a bead, a flat wooden pendant, a scrapbooking frame or inside an open geometric-shaped bead? Dare to be different!

1. Prepare image
Using the frame as your guide, trace around the desired image with a pencil. Cut the photo to fit the metal frame.

2. Adhere image to paper
Cut decorative paper to fit metal frames. Place a dot of gloss to adhere the photo to the decorative paper.

3. Add gloss
Insert the photo into the frame. Add gloss to the back of the frame.

4. SPREAD GLOSS

Use a paintbrush to spread the gloss and remove any bubbles. Let it dry for 24 hours.

5. ADD GLOSS TO FRONT

Add gloss to the front of the frame and let it dry. Remove bubbles as needed. Use the other end of the paintbrush to scoot the frame to a dry part of the lid. Let it dry completely, about 24 hours. It will be completely clear when dry.

TIP

The gloss may change the color of your paper.

6. ADD CHAIN

Open the link and attach the toggle clasp to the chain. Connect the toggle clasp and metal frame to the chain.

Tinsel Tree

As much as I love gorgeous, green pine trees, I am also drawn to sparkly silver trees. There is nothing like the glitter of silver tinsel with bright colorful lights reflecting from it. I wanted to create that sparkly kitschy feeling in these earrings. If the tree makes people smile, I hope the earrings will, too.

These earring are simple and quick to make. Go multicolored for a classic kitschy feel, or choose a favorite color so you can wear them all year long.

MATERIALS

2 4mm bicone crystals in desired color

2 6mm top-drilled crystal AB bicones

18 silver-lined clear bugle beads

8 silver headpins

4 eyepins

2 ear wires

6 6mm jump rings

TOOLS

needle-nose pliers

round-nose pliers

wire cutters

FINISHED LENGTH: 2½" (6cm)

GET INSPIRED!

I get excited when I see sparkly things. I can spot a speck of glitter from a few feet away! The next time you come across something shiny or sparkly, imagine how you can use it as inspiration. Ice crystals covering a windowpane, shimmering water droplets on a bright red rose, a pretty green margarita in a salt-rimmed glass—let the sparkles spark your imagination.

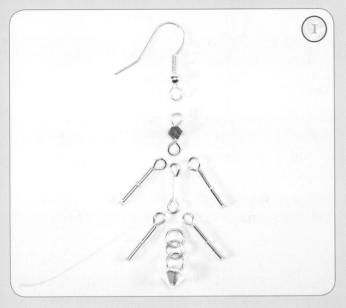

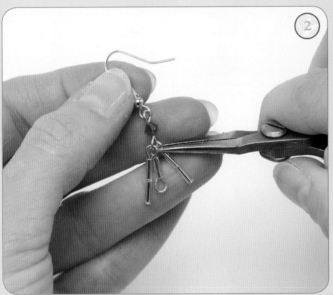

1. CREATE SECTIONS

Place two bugle beads each onto four headpins. Make a loop (see Making a Loop on page 13) and trim any excess wire.

Place a 4mm bicone onto an eyepin. Make a loop and trim any excess wire.

Place a bugle bead onto a headpin. Make a loop and trim any excess wire.

Open a jump ring (see Opening and Closing Jump Rings on page 15) and slide on a top-drilled crystal. Connect this jump ring to two other jump rings.

2. ATTACH FIRST SECTION

Attach the eyepin with the 4mm bicone to the ear wire. On the other loop, attach the eyepin with one bugle bead and two of the headpins with two bugle beads.

3. ATTACH SECOND SECTION

Beneath the bugle bead, add the remaining pieces: the jump ring dangle and the other two headpins with two bugle beads.

[5os Holiday Wreath]

My treasure-hunting hobby once revolved around finding kitschy items from the 1950s. My kitchen was decorated with an assortment of flea market finds, including a red formica table with red vinyl chairs. Salt and pepper shakers in the forms of TVs? But of course!

When I discovered a fun plastic wreath with silvery accents, I thought it made the perfect frame for a light-up Santa I had used in my Christmas decorating for years. I experimented with different materials to create this wreath as a bracelet, and finally settled on crinkle wire in this great green color. It seems to have just the right amount of kitschy spirit!

MATERIALS

Bracelet
- 12 8mm silver sparkle beads
- 16 5mm silver sparkle beads
- 40" (102cm) green crinkle wire
- 5-strand bar clasp
- 66 small crimp tubes

Dangle
- 1 Santa charm
- 3 6mm light siam red crystal bicones
- 2 4mm light siam red crystal bicones
- 1 silver lobster claw clasp
- 4 silver jump rings
- 2 silver headpins

TOOLS

wire cutters
needle-nose pliers
round-nose pliers

FINISHED LENGTH: 6½" (17cm)

GET INSPIRED!

Are you a collector? If you have at least three of the same or similar item, chances are you have those tendencies. Challenge yourself to design a piece of jewelry to represent one of your favorite collections. Whether it's bright tin toys from the 1930s or a Star Trek *collection, you'll have an extension of your favorite collection ready to wear any time.*

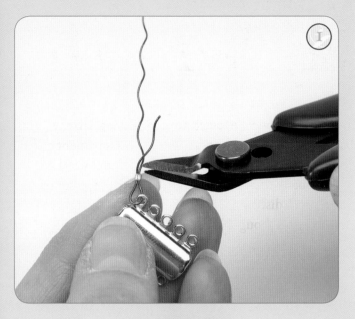

1. PREPARE WIRE PIECES
Cut five 8" (20cm) strands of crinkle wire. Attach each strand to the clasp by sliding a crimp bead onto the wire, sliding the wire through a hole in the clasp and back down through the crimp bead. Flatten the bead with needle-nose pliers (see Flattening Crimp Tubes on page 12). Use the wire cutters to trim any excess wire.

2. EMBELLISH WITH BEADS
Each bead will have a flattened crimp bead on either side of it in this pattern. Space the beads about 1" (3cm) apart.

3. ADD ONE BEAD PER INCH
Strands 1, 3 and 5: String on a 5mm bead, 5mm bead, 8mm bead, 5mm bead, 8mm bead and a 5mm bead.

Strands 2 and 4: String on a 5mm bead, 8mm bead, 8mm bead, 8mm bead and a 5mm bead.

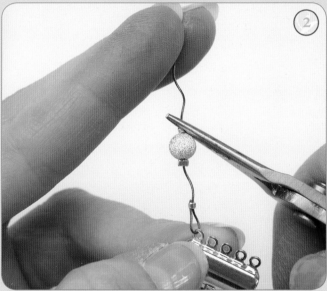

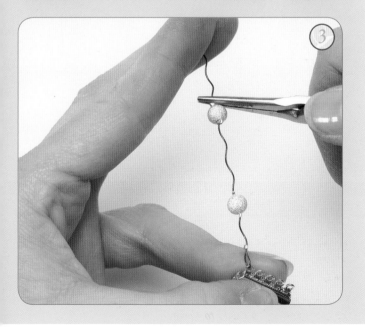

4. ADD JUMP RING

Add a jump ring to the last loop on the clasp.

5. CREATE DANGLE

Connect three jump ring links (see Opening and Closing Jump Rings on page 15) and attach to the Santa charm.

Attach a lobster claw clasp to the top jump ring.

Add a 4mm crystal and two 6mm crystals to a head-pin. Add a 4mm crystal and a 6mm crystal to a second headpin. Make loops on both (see Making a Loop on page 13) and trim any excess wire.

Open the jump ring attached to the lobster claw clasp and add one beaded headpin on either side of the Santa charm. Close the jump ring.

6. ADD DANGLE

Attach the lobster claw clasp to the jump ring on the bracelet.

Variation: 50s Holiday Wreath Earrings

This crinkle wire is such a fun and unique material, using it in a pair of coordinating earrings was a must!

MATERIALS

2 8mm silver sparkle beads

2 5mm silver sparkle beads

10" (25cm) green crinkle wire

2 large ear wires

4 large crimp tubes

ASSEMBLE EARRINGS

Cut two 5" (13cm) strands of crinkle wire.

Take each strand through an ear wire loop and bring the ends together.

Add a large crimp bead, 8mm bead, 5mm bead and a large crimp bead.

Flatten the crimp tubes with needle-nose pliers.

Variation: Interchangeable Dangle

This bracelet and earring set is so light and airy that you might want to wear it during other seasons besides the winter holidays. You can easily turn this holiday wreath into a summer piece by removing the Santa dangle and replacing it with a sparkly green and silver dangle.

MATERIALS

1 5mm silver sparkle bead

1 6mm emerald bicone crystal

1 silver spacer bead

1 silver-tone lobster claw clasp

1 silver-tone headpin

4 silver-tone jump rings

ASSEMBLE DANGLE

Add a 6mm bicone, silver spacer and a 5mm silver sparkle bead to a headpin.

Make a loop and trim any excess wire.

Add four silver jump rings and attach a silver lobster claw clasp to the top ring.

Festive Packages

I love making jewelry as gifts and taking time to package it nicely. As I design and construct the jewelry, I find myself filled with happy thoughts and memories of that person. These earrings represent the gift-giving experience and the idea of a tiny package holding a handmade piece of jewelry.

These beads were a great find and exactly what I needed to turn the little packages into earrings. Matching the beads was a lot like matching wrapping paper with bows!

MATERIALS

Silver Earrings
2 10mm silver-tone cubes
2 6mm topaz bicone crystals
2 clear E beads
2 silver-tone headpins
2 silver-tone eyepins
2 large silver-tone ear wires

Gold Earrings
2 10mm gold-tone cubes
2 gold-tone E beads
2 6mm golden yellow bicone crystals
2 gold-tone headpins
2 gold-tone eyepins
2 gold-tone ear wires

TOOLS
wire cutters
needle-nose pliers

FINISHED LENGTH:
silver: 2" (5cm)
gold: 1¾" (4cm)

GET INSPIRED!

I love reading how-to books and checking out crafty websites to gather unique, new techniques and materials for gift wrapping. A well-embellished gift package is similar to wearing festive and sparkly jewelry. The next time you give a gift, create a piece of jewelry to resemble the gift packaging and attach it for extra sparkle. This addition will not be forgotten.

1. CREATE SECTIONS FOR SILVER EARRINGS

Add a cube and an E bead to a headpin. Make a loop (see Making a Loop on page 13) and trim any excess wire.

Add a 6 mm topaz bicone to an eyepin. Make a loop and trim any excess wire.

2. ATTACH BOTTOM SECTIONS

Using the needle-nose pliers, connect the bottom two pieces of the earring.

3. ADD EAR WIRE

Connect the ear wire to the other loop on the topaz bicone eyepin. Repeat Steps 1–3 for the second earring.

4. CREATE GOLD EARRINGS

Follow Steps 1–3 to create the gold earrings.

Resources

Trolling the aisles of your favorite local bead shops and craft stores is always a fabulous option for finding inspiration.

TOHO BEADS
seed beads
www.tohobeads.net

DRITZ
interfacing
www.dritz.com

FIRE MOUNTAIN GEMS
beads, tolls wire and findings
www.firemountaingems.com

OFFRAY
ribbon
www.offray.com

BLUE MOON BEADS
beads and charms
www.bluemoonbeads.com

PLAID
beads, findings and paints
www.plaidonline.com

SOFT FLEX
beads, findings and wires
www.softflexcompany.com

SWAROVSKI CRYSTALS
crystals, gems and beads
www.swarovski.com

ACCU-FLEX
beading wires
www.accuflexwire.com

HIRSCHBERT SCHUTZ & CO., INC.
Horizon Group USA
beads and findings
www.horizongroupusa.com

COUSIN
beads, findings and tools
www.cousin.com

BLUMENTHAL LANSING COMPANY
buttons, sewing and general craft supplies
www.blumenthallansing.com

DARICE
general craft supplies
www.darice.com

TRIMTEX
ribbons and trims
www.trimtex.com

JHB INTERNATIONAL
buttons
www.buttons.com

MAKING MEMORIES
scrapbook papers and supplies
www.makingmemories.com

DECOART
Triple Thick Glaze
www.decoart.com

HALCRAFT USA
beads and pendants
www.halcraft.com

Index

Get inspired with these other fine North Light Books

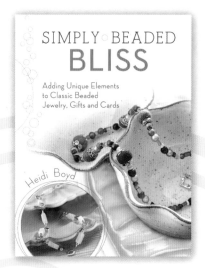

SIMPLY BEADED BLISS
BY HEIDI BOYD

Break away from the everyday bead-and-string combo with *Simply Beaded Bliss*. In this book, you'll learn how to incorporate mixed-media elements including paper, sequins, miniature toys and even fishing tackle into your jewelry. You'll discover how to use fingernail polish to create the look of enamel and how to link basic snaps to form the core of a charm bracelet. Choose from over 50 simple projects that combine classic beading techniques with mixed-media elements—all with Heidi Boyd's signature simply beautiful style.

ISBN-10: 1-60061-095-1
ISBN-13: 978-1-60061-095-0
PAPERBACK, 128 PAGES, Z2004

THE IMPATIENT BEADER GETS INSPIRED
BY MARGOT POTTER

Don't be afraid—get out there and find your inner art girl. You have terrific jewelry designs in your head just itching to get out. In a follow-up to her first beading book, jewelry designer Margot Potter gives you 40 sassy step-by-step jewelry projects plus the know-how you need to springboard off of her designs and create your own customized pieces. You'll also get regular visits from cartoon Margot, in outfits that match the theme of each chapter. Watch out for the item that inspired each piece--and don't be surprised if you get some ideas of your own.

ISBN-10: 1-58180-854-2
ISBN-13: 978-1-58180-854-4
PAPERBACK, 128 PAGES, Z0109

BEYOND BEADING BASICS
BY CAROLE RODGERS

Take your beading skills to the next level as you go *Beyond Beading Basics*. Conquer the more complex aspects of beading, such as using common bead findings as integral parts of your designs, using multiple-hole beads, making baskets and other shapes with wire and beads and how to combine stitches to achieve unique effects. Carole Rodgers offers you more than 25 projects and an equal number of techniques to launch you into bead artistry.

ISBN-10: 1-89689-925-X
ISBN-13: 978-0-89689-925-4
PAPERBACK, 144 PAGES, Z3628

These and other fine North Light Books are available at your local craft retailer, bookstore or online supplier, or visit our Web site at www.mycraftivitystore.com.